"*St. Faustina Prayer Book for the C*
needed treasure which allows us to g
his call to conversion. I pray that a
touched by God's love and experien
Jesus more closely as his disciples."

— CARDINAL SEÁN PATRICK O'MALLEY, O.F.M. CAP.
Archbishop of Boston

"In her most recent book, Susan Tassone — our very own 'Apostle for the Souls in Purgatory' — uses the spiritual wisdom of St. Faustina to call us all to conversion. Use it faithfully to pray for relatives and friends, and apply it to yourself to help with your own growth in holiness."

— GREG ERLANDSON
Editor in Chief, Catholic News Service

"Following her many valuable books on the holy souls in purgatory, Susan Tassone's *St. Faustina Prayer Book for the Conversion of Sinners* involves three of my favorite topics: St. Faustina, mercy, and conversion. This is a great book to help you pray for others, but it's more than that. Filled with prayers and inspiration for the continual, day-by-day conversion of our own hearts, it's a book for each one of us."

— VINNY FLYNN
Author of *Mercy's Gaze*

"Each of us is called to become a saint. Once we hear the call of God, experience the pulsating love of the divine, and surrender every facet of our life and personality to the Lord, nothing can ever be the same again. Susan Tassone's latest book, *St. Faustina Prayer Book for the Conversion of Sinners*, can greatly assist in the continual conversion of heart, mind, and soul needed to wholeheartedly respond to this universal call to holiness. The plethora of prayers, devotions, and spiritual practices this book contains can help the reader to obtain the graces needed for a deeper commitment to Christ for oneself, one's loved ones, and the entire world."

— MOST REVEREND DONALD J. HYING
Bishop of Gary, Indiana

"In her — excellent — *St. Faustina Prayer Book for the Conversion of Sinners*, author Susan Tassone examines and explains the interdependence of all of us in God's plan of salvation: how we play a role not only in our own conversion but in the conversion of others. As always, Susan never loses sight of the way this 'vocation' includes praying for the holy souls in purgatory, just as Our Lady instructed the young children at Fatima in 1917. Charity was the essence of Mary's message to them when she asked that they work for the conversion of sinners through prayer and sacrifice. It remains her message to us."

— DAVID M. CAROLLO
Executive Director, World Apostolate of Fatima

"In the Gospel, Our Lord instructs that some types of spiritual conversion can only be accomplished by prayer and fasting. Susan Tassone's *St. Faustina Prayer Book for the Conversion of Sinners* provides us a wonderful resource to help focus one's prayer to complement one's fasting. I highly recommend it for those seriously wanting to 'live the fast' and convert hearts and souls to Christ!"

— ANDREW LaVALLEE
Founder and Director, Live the Fast

"In these secular times that relish personal autonomy as the rudder of life, we are tempted to relish and even boast about our sins. Concepts of conversion, mercy, penance, and forgiveness are hard to digest in this age. Susan Tassone offers a compendium here that brings forth from the Church's treasury of prayers and self-examen contributions on these subjects by select saints with Sister Faustina Kowalska's mystical intuitions as centerpiece. This work invites a contemporary generation to revisit the Church's proclamation of the infinite mercy and love of Jesus Christ. With citations from the Marian appearances appealing for the conversion of souls, this book will assist the pious soul to explore more deeply the freeing experience of conversion and an encounter with the mercy of God that can penetrate the cynicism of the age and draw the soul closer to the person of Jesus Christ."

— MOST REVEREND JOSEPH N. PERRY
Auxiliary Bishop, Archdiocese of Chicago

"Once again Susan Tassone has taken the *Diary* of St. Faustina and culled gems that could be overlooked by even an expert on this saint's spirituality. (When St. Faustina tells of her efforts to effect a change in her sister, Wanda, I think of all the people for whom I've ever prayed.) Susan's superior writings on St. Faustina's spirituality can help us each grow in holiness as we attempt to become a channel of God's mercy for others."

— Father Dan Cambra, M.I.C.

Holy Souls Sodality at

The National Shrine of The Divine Mercy

"Susan Tassone's *St. Faustina Prayer Book for the Conversion of Sinners* is a must-read! It not only will inspire you but renew your faith in the unfathomable mercy of God. Do yourself a favor: read this book, share it with others, and trust in the power of God's mercy to bring about conversion even of the most hardened heart."

— Drew Mariani

Host of the nationally syndicated

radio program, "The Drew Mariani Show"

St. Faustina Prayer Book
for the Conversion of Sinners

Susan Tassone

Our Sunday Visitor

www.osv.com
Our Sunday Visitor Publishing Division
Our Sunday Visitor, Inc.
Huntington, Indiana 46750

Nihil Obstat
Msgr. Michael Heintz, Ph.D.
Censor Librorum

Imprimatur
✠ Kevin C. Rhoades
Bishop of Fort Wayne-South Bend
November 23, 2016

The *Nihil Obstat* and *Imprimatur* are official declarations that a book is free from doctrinal or moral error. It is not implied that those who have granted the *Nihil Obstat* and *Imprimatur* agree with the contents, opinions, or statements expressed.

Selections from St. Faustina's *Diary* are copyright © The Association of Marian Helpers. Used by permission. All rights reserved.

Every reasonable effort has been made to determine copyright holders of excerpted materials and to secure permissions as needed. If any copyrighted materials have been inadvertently used in this work without proper credit being given in one form or another, please notify Our Sunday Visitor in writing so that future printings of this work may be corrected accordingly.

Our Sunday Visitor Publishing Division, Our Sunday Visitor, Inc.,
200 Noll Plaza, Huntington, IN 46750; 1-800-348-2440

ISBN: 978-1-68192-066-5 (Inventory No. T1815)
eISBN: 978-1-68192-071-9
LCCN: 2016962101

Cover design: Amanda Falk
Cover image: *The Lord of Mercy* statue, St. John Cantius Church, Chicago;
photo by Garrett Fosco
Cover background: Shutterstock
Interior composition: Dianne Nelson
Interior design: Sherri L. Hoffman

PRINTED IN THE UNITED STATES OF AMERICA

Dearest Jesus, who takes away the sins of the world,
have mercy on those we love.

—

TABLE OF CONTENTS

Editor's note: Citations at the end of quotations refer to number sections of the *Diary of St. Maria Faustina Kowalska*. For example, see "(1372)" on page 24.

Personal Acknowledgments

I'm so pleased and happy to tell you about these incredible people who helped make this book possible.

To Bert Ghezzi: Thank you, exceptional editor, for giving structure to another best seller and for allowing me the freedom to be as creative as possible.

To Bill Dodds: My extraordinary and special copy editor, who always make my books more powerful, warm, and eloquent. Thank you for helping readers of this book better see conversion through the eyes of kindness and compassion.

To Father Dan Cambra, M.I.C.: I can't thank you enough for telling me no one had written about St. Faustina's *Diary* while looking through the lens of conversion! What a glorious sight it is to see her beautiful words come into focus that way. Thanks to you, I can share them with others. Her message of God's mercy continues to reach hearts, minds, and souls around the world because of what you do.

To my former editor and still dear friend, Jackie Lindsey: This is our tenth book together, and none of them could have happened without you!

To Steven Jay Gross: There will never be enough words in this world or the next to describe you or to thank you. You are the greatest blessing in my life. I became "The Purgatory Lady" because of you, my dear, dear friend, and I thank God for you daily.

To Deacon Mike McCloskey: I can't even begin to tell you how helpful you've been. I hope you know I'm deeply grateful — and so fortunate! — to have you as a friend.

To Larry Lesof: You're always there for me, dear friend. Always helpful. Always faithful. My eternal thanks.

To Mike Wick: Many authors have a "go-to-guy." You're my "go-to-guy extraordinaire"!

To George Foster: Thank you for going over my manuscripts with such amazing attention to so many, many details!

To Loyola University Chicago librarians Yolanda Wersching and Vanessa Crouther: And yet *again*, your assistance was outstanding! And so appreciated.

To Maria Cristina Ramis and Kathryn Owens: I'm sure no other author has a better resource than you two for tracking down just the resources my books need! Thank you, wonderfully resourceful ladies.

To Theresa Leurck: You're not only a champion of EWTN but my champion for all you do for the holy souls in purgatory.

To Frank Scharl: You are my treasured friend, with such a generous heart, who shows up like a guardian angel to help me. The holy souls and I thank you.

To Garrett Fosco: Thank you so, so much for a cover photo that captured the spirit — *and truth!* — of what this book is all about.

FOREWORD

Helping Jesus Find "The One" Who Is Lost by Helping "The One" Who Is Lost Find Jesus

There's no doubt why Jesus came into the world: "To seek and to save the lost" (Lk 19:10). To save all of us. To save you. To save me.

He was and is the Good Shepherd, willing to leave the ninety-nine sheep in the wasteland and follow the lost sheep until He finds it. Then, rejoicing, carrying it home on His shoulders and returning it to His flock.

God doesn't want any of His wayward children to be lost, but truly rejoices when they repent of their sins, turn back to Him, and are saved. This is conversion.

In her latest book, *St. Faustina Prayer Book for the Conversion of Sinners*, Susan Tassone clearly explains the nature of conversion and the dynamics involved. Jesus wants all of us, each of us, to be involved in His mission of universal salvation. In other words, we must help bring souls to Him by our prayers, sacrifices, good example, works of mercy, and efforts at evangelization. This, along with growth in personal holiness, has always been a major focus in living our Christian lives. The famous saying of St. John Bosco, founder of the Salesian Congregation, sums this up: "Give me souls; you can have the rest!"

It's evident, though, that as the world becomes more materialistic (focusing only on things one wants in this world), more hedonistic (seeking sexual pleasures of all kinds despite God's law and commandments), and more proud and arrogant (developing a pompous attitude of being self-sufficient and not needing God), conversion will become an increasingly major focus of the Church's mission, and for each of us personally.

Even now as a priest, people often ask me: "Father, please pray for my children who refuse to go to Mass anymore … for my son who is living with his girlfriend … for my daughter who wants to marry her girlfriend … for my grandchildren who are on drugs … for my sister's daughter who wants to get an abortion … for my friends, who have four children and are getting a divorce…." The list is endless.

Those for whom these prayers are requested are, ultimately, living lives of great unhappiness, but, infinitely worse, they're in grave danger of being separated from God for all eternity. What can be done to save them? Here Susan Tassone's book gives us solid guidance.

In our own time, we've seen Pope Francis focus on mercy and conversion of hearts, with special emphasis during the 2015-2016 Extraordinary Jubilee of Mercy. His message for all of us is the one St. Faustina received from Jesus. The one Our Lord entrusted to her. The one she recorded so faithfully in her diary.

And what St. Faustina teaches us echoes the words of Our Lady in Fátima, Portugal, a century ago. When Mary appeared to three shepherd children — Lúcia, Francisco, and Jacinta — she told them: "Pray, pray very much, and make sacrifices for sinners, for many souls go to hell, because there are none to sacrifice themselves and to pray for them."

Conversion has never been very easy, but it's always been crucial. The soul of the person converted will be saved from eternal death and punishment. And(!) the one who helps the sinner convert will share in his or her glory in heaven. Above all, God himself will be glorified by those who have been saved. As Jesus told St. Faustina, "I expect from you, My child, a great number of souls who will glorify My mercy for all eternity" (1489).

The conversions of an individual (a family member, a friend, and even an enemy) usually takes perseverance and sacrifice. One of the greatest examples is the conversion of St. Augustine by the prayers and tears of his mother, St. Monica. Augustine was caught up in a life of lust, having lived with two women and fathered a child by one of them. Even when he came to the point where he wanted to give up his sinful ways, he felt helpless to resist his passions. His devout mother prayed her heart out for him. She went to the church twice a day, morning and evening, for sixteen years. Finally, her prayers, her pleas, were answered. And what a conversion that was! Because of her trust in God's mercy and her incredible dedication to praying for her son, St. Monica became an example of trust and hope for those who pray for the conversion of loved ones. Thank God, there are many "modern Monicas" in our Church today!

Yes, St. Monica's example can be intimidating but it's important to keep in mind that praying for conversions in general — for a most-needy sinner, for a sinner who will die today, for someone who has drifted, or stormed, away from the Church — requires simply that we pray. We can have confidence that Jesus in His Divine Mercy will hear our prayers and apply them to whom He wishes. Only in heaven will we know the effectiveness of our prayers for sinners when we share the Lord's joy, when we rejoice, with those whom our prayers have helped.

Thank you, Susan Tassone, for writing this book. Thank you for a guide that will inspire many to pray and sacrifice for the "one sheep" who is lost.

— Father Andrew Apostoli, CFR

INTRODUCTION

Calling You Home

Dear Friends,

You might be surprised at how often St. Faustina, the Patroness of Divine Mercy, wrote about conversion. I was.

In page after page and chapter after chapter, her *Diary* speaks of Jesus' call for the conversion of sinners.

But what did "conversion" mean to St. Faustina? And to Our Lord? And how do we each take that message, that meaning, and apply it — no, more than that — how do we come to *live* it, page after page and chapter after chapter, in the book of our *own* life? How do we become more faithful in praying for the conversions of our relatives, friends, and others?

That's what *St. Faustina Prayer Book for the Conversion of Sinners* is all about. That's what life on earth, and time in purgatory, are all about.

Time and again, you sin. Time and again, I sin. Time and again, Jesus calls each of us to turn, to return, to our Heavenly Father and do His will.

Today Jesus is calling you to conversion. Calling you to sainthood. Calling you home.

You, and the souls of your dearly departed, are in my prayers.

— Susan

PART ONE
Conversion

I. What Is Conversion?

"The time is fulfilled, and the kingdom of God is at hand;
repent, and believe in the gospel."
— Mark 1:15

In one of his first interviews after being elected pontiff, Pope Francis was asked to describe himself. "I am a sinner," he said.

Four words that shocked the world but shouldn't have.

Every pope has been a sinner.

Every human being — except Jesus and His mother, Mary — has been a sinner.

So a prayer book focusing on "the conversion of sinners" isn't just about "them": the big-time, notorious sinners. It's about us: the little-time, often slow-to-correct-our-faults, sinners.

Members of both categories need our prayers. And we need the prayers of others.

———

It wouldn't be hard to come up with a list of the horrible and harmful activities of the big-time sinners. Abortionists, pornographers, sex traffickers, child abusers, dictators, and on and on. But what about the little-time sinners? Really now. Aren't they, aren't we, doing pretty much okay?

Not according to St. Bernard of Clairvaux, who told his community: "There are more people converted from mortal sin to grace than there are religious converted from good to better."

Yes, he was speaking about members of religious communities, but certainly the same could be said of those who consider themselves religious: those who take their Catholicism seriously and live good and holy lives.

Lives that, St. Bernard was saying, could be better ... and holier.

That's what conversion is. For some, it's getting out of the pornography business. For others, it's moving away from those favorite little vices that, over the years, have held us back from the person God is calling us to be.

As you may know, the word "convert" comes from the Latin meaning to turn (*vertere*) together with (*con* or *cum*). We're facing one way, we're heading down a path in this direction, but — with someone else — we turn in a new, and better, direction. We head down a new, and better, path. Or, more accurately, we do that with Someone else. We turn with the One who continually calls us to conversion because we continually need it.

Here's another way to look at it. You've probably heard the expression "a heart of stone." Mortal sin piled on mortal sin over years and years has turned the big-time sinner's heart to stone.

But what's the small-time sinner's heart like? Perhaps like a lump of modeling clay that's been left out and untouched for too long. It's hard and brittle. It crumbles easily and can't be formed, or transformed, into anything.

What is conversion? A modern dictionary says it's this: "to change (something) into a different form or so that it can be used in a different way."

To change a heart. To change a mind. To change a soul. A heart that loves more. A mind that longs for greater knowledge of, and intimacy, with its Creator. A soul that seeks holiness by, day after day, seeking God's will and striving to live it.

What Does Conversion Require?

Draw near to God and he will draw near to you. Cleanse your hands,
you sinners, and purify your hearts.... Humble yourselves before the
Lord and he will exalt you.
— James 4:8, 10

What does conversion require? The short answer is: God and you.

You can't do it without Him. And He won't do it without you. (You always have free will.)

But that short answer doesn't mean it's a simple answer.

Conversion requires prayer ... and prayer requires conversion. It isn't a "one-and-done" proposition. It's a daily process. More than that, it can be multiple decisions and actions within one day. Day after day till death. Why? Because it's answering God's constant call for us to change our mind and our heart: a lifetime of His inviting you and me to become a saint.

How do we do that? First, to use a common and contemporary expression, "Ya gotta want it!" There are no "accidental saints."

There's no doubt, St. Faustina had that deep, deep desire.

She told Our Lord: "You know that from my earliest years I have wanted to become a great saint; that is to say, I have wanted to love You with a love so great that there would be no soul who has hitherto loved You so" (1372).

The comforting, and disturbing, truth is that we have everything St. Faustina had in order for us to become saints too. God offers the grace to do just that. We have "only" to take Him up on His offer and use His freely given gift.

You and I can become a saint. And there's a bonus! In the same way, we can avoid purgatory too.

There's no magical formula, but there is a mystical one: we can seek the grace of conversion through prayer — and, through prayer, we can better and better live that grace. But as we all know, prayer can be far from easy. It demands time and effort. And a deeper conversion, a stronger conversion, often means more time. More effort. It calls for an increasing surrender to God *and* an abandonment of selfishness, which is the core of sin and an impediment to prayer.

"Impossible!" you might say. But apparently not. Others have done it. The Church has a whole canon — a list — of those she has declared saints, and there are countless other souls in heaven whose names we don't know and won't know until we join them there.

But no saint started out as a saint. Each person converted his or her life, day by day. Many, if not most, began that journey with "baby steps." That's more good news because we can do the same. And that's all God asks. For today.

Step, step, misstep. Step, step, fall. Step, step … step.

Over time, with effort and grace, our steps become surer, our stride becomes longer, and our endurance increases.

And as we grow closer to God, the closer still we want to be. We become better aware of our imperfections — those nagging missteps and falls — and we want to eliminate them. Saints weren't being falsely modest when they declared themselves to be sinners. Sometimes big-time sinners. And yet, again with time and effort, with the grace of God and the choices they made, they grew in holiness. But as they did so, they came to realize that they needed to become even more deeply converted if they wanted to better do God's will for them — and to better answer His call, His invitation, to follow the unique and incredible path He was using to lead them home to Him for all eternity.

CONFORMING TO GOD'S WAYS

It wasn't just through deepening prayer that St. Faustina sought the will of God, but also through living in conformity to God's ways. If our prayers are converting us, then we may well be surprised to realize that, as with St. Faustina's prayers, they're starting to bear spiritual fruit, including:

- Greater acts of generosity
- Mercy
- Patience
- Humble service
- Faith
- Having a devotion to Our Lady, following her example and putting ourselves under the mantle of her protection (by praying the Rosary)
- Frequenting the sacraments (Mass and Reconciliation)
- Living a Christian life in conformity with the Gospel
- Doing works of charity
- Forgiving our enemies

How Does St. Faustina View Conversion?

Pray at all times in the Spirit, with all prayer, and supplication.
To that end keep alert with all perseverance,
making supplication for all the saints.
— EPHESIANS 6:18

St. Faustina's main mission was helping Jesus save sinners, helping the dying, and releasing souls in purgatory. Her compassion for sinners was her life, as she made atonement for them and incessantly pleaded for God to show His mercy on them.

She had no doubt He would. "And fear nothing, dear soul, whoever you are," she wrote. "The greater the sinner, the greater his right to Your mercy, O Lord. O incomprehensible Goodness! God is the first to stoop to the sinner" (598).

Clearly, St. Faustina understood that conversion applies to everyone, no matter how low we may go, no matter what heights our souls may attain. There's always room for improvement because there's always room for more grace, for deeper conversion, and for growing closer to perfection itself: that is, for closer to God.

AN ETERNAL LIFE-CHANGING PRAYER FOR OTHERS

"Today Jesus said to me, I desire that you know more profoundly the love that burns in My Heart for souls, and you will understand this when you meditate upon My Passion. Call upon My mercy on behalf of sinners; I desire their salvation. When you say this prayer, with a contrite heart and with faith on behalf of some sinner, I will give him the grace of conversion. This is the prayer:

'O Blood and Water, which gushed forth from the Heart of Jesus as a fount of Mercy for us, I trust in You.'" (187)

Coupled with our own growth is the conversion of others. Just as Jesus allowed St. Faustina to do, He lets us play a role in helping others to turn with Him, to walk with Him. Sometimes this is through our prayers and sacrifices, and sometimes through that spiritual fruit that isn't meant for us alone but to be shared, in so many ways, with others.

What were the first steps for St. Faustina?

Prayer. If we don't pray, then we can't say we're on the way to being converted — or perhaps, more accurately, on the path of conversion. We can't claim we're falling deeper in love with God. And, it may well be, until we begin and manage to take a few steps, we can't imagine we would *want* to deepen that relationship — or have a clue of what joy that deepening would bring.

Prayer is the language of this *conversion*, this conversation with our Creator. It's one way we respond to His courting us. Conversion is falling *in love* with God.

What Does Purgatory Have to Do with Conversion?

"Not my will, but thine, be done."
— LUKE 22:42

What's the chief way to avoid purgatory? Doing the will of God in all things in the present moment. What's conversion? Striving to get better at doing his will.

That theme runs throughout St. Faustina's diary:

My sanctity and perfection consist in the close union of my will with the will of God. God never violates our free will. It is up to us whether we want to receive God's grace or not. It is up to us whether we will cooperate with it or waste it. (1107)

O Jesus, I want to live in the present moment, to live as if this were the last day of my life. I want to use every moment scrupulously for the greater glory of God, to use every circumstance for the benefit of my soul. I want to look upon everything, from the point of view that nothing happens without the will of God. (1183)

The hearts of the holy souls in purgatory beat in perfect harmony with the will of God. The holy souls *want us* to convert and become holy here on earth.

Let our prayer be that of Our Lord and Our Lady: "Thy will be done." Conforming ourselves to the plan of God will give us the grace to avoid purgatory.

We are required to do penance for our sins to make satisfaction in this world. What are these means of satisfaction? Devotion to the Mother of God; charity toward the living and deceased; mortification and faithfulness to our state in life; reception of the sacraments; confidence in the divine mercy of God; and death in union with Jesus.

We are invited to be one with the holy souls in their love, their eager expiation, and their union with God. One with them in purifying our hearts from imperfections, in atoning for our sins, in learning something new of the incomprehensible holiness of God. Becoming one with those who rest in the blissful vision of God.

II. What Is Penance?

*If my people who are called by my name humble themselves, and pray
and seek my face, and turn from their wicked ways, then I will hear
from heaven, and will forgive their sin and heal their land.*
— 2 Chronicles 7:14

We have a pretty clear idea of what's meant by the word "prayer," but what about "penance," as it's used when talking about conversion? This is how the glossary of the *Catechism of the Catholic Church* defines it:

> *Interior* penance: a conversion of heart toward God and away from sin, which implies the intention to change one's life because of hope in divine mercy (1431). *External* acts of penance include fasting, prayer, and almsgiving (1434). [Emphasis in original.]

So what we're talking about here isn't the Sacrament of Penance and Reconciliation. We'll get to that a little later.

Yes, penance is something we can do for the conversion of others, including those with hardened hearts, but it's also something we can do for ourselves. And while it always involves making a personal sacrifice, it can be "easy" in the sense that we never have to go far to do it. Opportunities are available every day, right in our own backyard. No, closer than that. We don't even have to leave the house.

Again, quoting the *Catechism of the Catholic Church*:

Jesus' call to conversion and penance, like that of the prophets before him, does not aim first at outward works, "sackcloth and ashes," fasting and mortification, but at the *conversion of the heart, interior conversion*. Without this, such penances remain sterile and false; however, interior conversion urges expression in visible signs, gestures and works of penance.

Interior repentance is a radical reorientation of our whole life, a return, a conversion to God with all our heart, an end of sin, a turning away from evil, with repugnance toward the evil actions we have committed. At the same time it entails the desire and resolution to change one's life, with hope in God's mercy and trust in the help of his grace. This conversion of heart is accompanied by a salutary pain and sadness which the Fathers called *animi cruciatus* (affliction of spirit) and *compunctio cordis* (repentance of heart).

The human heart is heavy and hardened. God must give man a new heart. (nn. 1430-1432; emphasis in original)

So when it comes to acts of penance, in the words of Dorothy in the Land of Oz, "There's no place like home." Acts of penance can, and pretty much have to, begin right where we live and be directed toward those who live with us. That "radical reorientation" of our whole life won't even make it out the door if we don't begin being more charitable — kind, forgiving, patient, and all the rest — to those closest to us.

This is easy to agree with in theory — but, as we all know, often more than a little challenging in practice. Accepting those challenges and overcoming those challenges is penance.

This is the essence of conversion … and the essence of bypassing purgatory.

Purgatory, the Final Penance

It's important to remember, or to realize for the first time, that the holy souls in purgatory are concerned about the salvation of those of us still on earth, especially of their loved ones and friends. Their prayers help us recognize our faults so that we can understand the malice of sin.

The souls have a tremendous resolve in assisting us to become holy — that is, to do the will of God in the present moment — so that we find the direct path to heaven. They don't want us to have to attend this "school of conversion" called purgatory! (Better to be "homeschooled," to start now right in our own homes.) Through their prayers, they reproach us by inspirations of the Holy Spirit — that's so, especially when we lose focus of what should be the vision of our path to holiness.

If we submit ourselves to their influence, we can avoid purgatory. Theirs is the spirit of penance, detesting all sin, having an ardent desire to satisfy justice with perfect resignation and humility. Each of us — you and I — need to imitate them. And we're oh, so foolish when we don't.

THE GREAT MYSTERY OF THE MASS

In the words of St. Faustina: "Oh, what awesome mysteries take place during Mass! A great mystery is accomplished in the Holy Mass. With what great devotion should we listen to and take part in this death of Jesus. One day we will know what God is doing for us in each Mass, and what sort of gift He is preparing in it for us. Only His divine love could permit that such a gift be provided for us" (914).

In this two-way relationship between the Church Militant and the Church Suffering (those of us on earth and the souls in purgatory), how can we help *them*? Through our sacrifices and prayers — and most especially through the Mass.

A living person is still capable of growing in sanctifying grace. And so a Mass offered for a person already in God's grace has the effect of giving the gift of increased grace, which the person may willingly receive in order to become more Christlike.

As an intercessory prayer, a Mass offered for a person in a state of actual mortal sin may yet supply the grace necessary for repentance, even though conversion is always a free acceptance of the grace that is offered.

The Mass is the most powerful gift we can give ourselves and our deceased loved ones. (As I've written in my previous books, I urge you to put Gregorian Masses in your wills. They are thirty consecutive Masses offered for one deceased soul. Pope St. Gregory popularized this devotion. (See the "Resources" chapter for more information.)

What Is Confession?

"Your sins are forgiven."
— LUKE 7:48

St. Faustina wrote that Jesus told her this about the sacrament of confession:

> Write, speak of My mercy. Tell souls where they are to look for solace;
> that is, in the Tribunal of Mercy [the Sacrament of Reconciliation]
> There the greatest miracles take place [and] are incessantly repeated.
> To avail oneself of this miracle, it is not necessary to go on a great
> pilgrimage or to carry out some external ceremony; it suffices to come
> with faith to the feet of My representative and to reveal to him one's

misery, and the miracle of Divine Mercy will be fully demonstrated. Were a soul like a decaying corpse so that from a human standpoint, there would be no [hope of] restoration and everything would already be lost, it is not so with God. The miracle of Divine Mercy restores that soul in full. Oh, how miserable are those who do not take advantage of the miracle of God's mercy! You will call out in vain, but it will be too late. (1448)

The *Catechism of the Catholic Church* points out that the sacrament has a number of names, each important in describing what it truly is and does:

It is called the *sacrament of conversion* because it makes sacramentally present Jesus' call to conversion, the first step in returning to the Father from whom one has strayed by sin.

It is called the *sacrament of Penance*, since it consecrates the Christian sinner's personal and ecclesial steps of conversion, penance, and satisfaction.

It is called the *sacrament of confession*, since the disclosure or confession of sins to a priest is an essential element of this sacrament. In a profound sense, it is also a "confession" — acknowledgment and praise — of the holiness of God and of his mercy toward sinful man.

It is called the *sacrament of forgiveness*, since by the priest's sacramental absolution God grants the penitent "pardon and peace."

It is called the *sacrament of Reconciliation*, because it imparts to the sinner the love of God who reconciles: "Be reconciled to God." He who lives by God's merciful love is ready to respond to the Lord's call: "Go; first be reconciled to your brother." (nn. 1423-1424; emphasis in original)

And, the *Catechism* goes on to say:

Without being strictly necessary, confession of everyday faults (venial sins) is nevertheless strongly recommended by the Church. Indeed the regular confession of our venial sins helps us form our conscience, fight against evil tendencies, let ourselves be healed by Christ and progress in the life of the Spirit. By receiving more frequently through this sacrament the gift of the Father's mercy, we are spurred to be merciful as he is merciful. (n. 1458)

We become more like God as we walk with Him, as we walk where He calls us to walk.

A sincere confession always leads us toward a complete conversion, where the meaning of conversion is a change of one's entire life, actions, and beliefs to line up with God's will for us. For some, it's a slight shift in the course we were on. For others, it's a major change in direction, venturing into seemingly uncharted, and at times frightening waters. Slight or major, it's what every saint has done (some, including Paul, Augustine, and Francis of Assisi, quite famously).

This isn't to say conversion is just confessing mortal sins. (Although "just" that action is taking a tremendous step.) There's a wider scope or spectrum to this. The Gospel speaks of "metanoia," a change of mind and heart that every believer must seek — and *live*. "Repent, and believe in the gospel" (Mk 1:15).

What's the Difference Between Penance and Repentance?

Penance always implies a renouncement, to give up something or put it aside voluntarily. It's something we choose to do, not something we're forced to do. (Again, free will plays a central role here.)

Give up what? Perhaps a small "creature comfort" (that daily latte). Put aside what? Maybe a (deeply ingrained) me-first attitude.

Why would we do something like that? Are we masochists? St. Paul has the answer:

> But I say, walk by the Spirit, and do not gratify the desires of the flesh. For the desires of the flesh are against the Spirit, and the desires of the Spirit are against the flesh; for these are opposed to each other, to prevent you from doing what you would. But if you are led by the Spirit you are not under the law. Now the works of the flesh are plain: immorality, impurity, licentiousness, idolatry, sorcery, enmity, strife, jealousy, anger, selfishness, dissension, party spirit [factions], envy, drunkenness, carousing, and the like. I warn you, as I warned you before, that those who do such things shall not inherit the kingdom of God. But the fruit of the Spirit is love, joy, peace, patience, kindness, goodness, faithfulness, gentleness, self-control; against such there is no law. And those who belong to Christ Jesus have crucified the flesh with its passions and desires.
>
> If we live by the Spirit, let us also walk by the Spirit. (Gal 5:16-25)

To use a modern idiom: We have to walk the talk! That, in a nutshell, is true repentance. That's true metanoia.

Fortunately, blessedly, God is always kind, merciful, and generous. Our Creator knows what we need and He offers it to us ("offers" doesn't force on us). He offers us grace through the sacrament of confession.

Here's more of what Jesus told St. Faustina about confession:

> Daughter, when you go to confession, to this fountain of My mercy, the Blood and Water which came forth from My Heart always flows down upon your soul and ennobles it. Every time you go to confession, immerse yourself entirely in My mercy, with great trust, so that I may pour the bounty of My grace upon your soul. When you ap-

proach the confessional, know this, that I Myself am waiting there for you. I am only hidden by the priest, but I Myself act in your soul. Here the misery of the soul meets the God of mercy. Tell souls that from this fount of mercy souls draw graces solely with the vessel of trust. If their trust is great, there is no limit to My generosity. The torrents of grace inundate humble souls. The proud remain always in poverty and misery, because My grace turns away from them to humble souls. (1602)

How Do We Prepare for Confession?

If we confess our sins, he is faithful and just, and will forgive our sins and cleanse us from all unrighteousness.
— 1 JOHN 1:9

Not surprisingly, St. Faustina's *Diary* includes descriptions of how she prepared to go to confession, advice on how we can better prepare to make a good confession, and comments on the sacrament in general. She wrote:

I will call to mind the Passion of Jesus at each confession, to arouse my heart to contrition. (225)

… I must pray for each of my confessors, that he might obtain the light of the Holy Spirit…. (647)

Concerning Holy Confession. We should derive two kinds of profit from Holy Confession:
1. We come to confession to be healed;
2. We come to be educated — like a small child, our soul has constant need of education.

O my Jesus, I understand these words to their very depths, and I know from my own experience that, on its own strength, the soul will not go far; it will exert itself greatly and will do nothing for the glory of God; it will err continually, because our mind is darkened and does not know how to discern its own affairs. I shall pay special attention to two things: firstly, I will choose, in making my confession, that which humiliates me most, even if it be a trifle, but something that costs me much, and for that reason I will tell it; secondly, I will practice contrition, not only during confession, but during every self-examination, and I will arouse within myself an act of perfect contrition, especially when I am going to bed. One more word: a soul which sincerely wants to advance in perfection must observe strictly the advice given by the spiritual director. There is as much holiness as there is dependence. (377)

ST. FAUSTINA'S PRAYER
TO THE SACRED HEART FOR SINNERS

"O Jesus, eternal Truth, our Life, I call upon You and I beg Your mercy for poor sinners. O sweetest Heart of my Lord, full of pity and unfathomable mercy, I plead with You for poor sinners. O Most Sacred Heart, Fount of Mercy from which gush forth rays of inconceivable graces upon the entire human race, I beg of You light for poor sinners. O Jesus, be mindful of Your own bitter Passion and do not permit the loss of souls redeemed at so dear a price of Your most precious Blood. O Jesus, when I consider the great price of Your Blood, I rejoice at its immensity, for one drop alone would have been enough for the salvation of all sinners. Although sin is an abyss of wickedness and ingratitude, the price paid for us can never be equalled. Therefore, let every soul trust in the Passion of the Lord, and place its hope in His mercy. God will not deny His mercy to anyone. Heaven and earth may change, but God's mercy will never be exhausted. Oh, what immense joy burns in my heart when I contemplate Your incomprehensible goodness, O Jesus! I desire to bring all sinners to Your feet that they may glorify Your mercy throughout endless ages." (72)

III. Invoke the Holy Spirit!

When the day of Pentecost had come, they were all together in one place. And suddenly a sound came from heaven like the rush of a mighty wind, and it filled all the house where they were sitting. And there appeared to them tongues as of fire, distributed and resting on each one of them. And they were all filled with the Holy Spirit and began to speak in other tongues, as the Spirit gave them utterance.
— Acts 2:1-4

It's good to keep in mind that the apostles weren't completely converted when they heard Jesus' call and immediately joined Him. Even after His passion, death, and resurrection — and just before His ascension — they wanted to know, "Now are you going to restore the Kingdom of Israel?" (see Acts 1:6). Or, in other words, "*Now* are we going to get to be hotshots in Jerusalem and beyond?"

No. Not by a long shot.

"You shall receive power when the Holy Spirit has come upon you," Jesus told them. "And you shall be my witnesses in Jerusalem and in all Judea and Samaria and to the end of the earth" (Acts 1:8).

Witnesses. A word that meant martyrs.

They would preach and teach and heal and baptize. And, tradition says, all but John would be martyred (this is the same disciple to whom Jesus entrusted His mother).

So how did these "converts" who became Jesus' followers become "converts" who died for Him? Just as Jesus had promised them, they received power when the Holy Spirit came upon them.

This is the same Spirit who can, and does, come upon us with the power to help us convert at a deeper level — at a higher level — at a greater and more powerful level. And this is the same Spirit who helps us turn, keeps us pointed in the right direction, and guides us on the path of the Father's will for us.

In the words of St. Faustina: "Faithfulness to the inspirations of the Holy Spirit — that is the shortest route *[to holiness]*" (291). And, she said, a key to being aware of those inspirations (from the Latin for "breathe into") is to stop and be quiet. Or, to quote the psalmist: "Be still, and know that I am God" (Ps 46:10). Or, to put it more bluntly in today's language: Sit down and shut up!

> In addition to the vows *[taken by members of St. Faustina's religious order]*, I see one rule as most important. Although all the rules are important, I put this one in first place, and it is silence. Truly, if this rule were to be observed strictly, I would not worry about the others. Women are very fond of talking, but the Holy Spirit does not speak to a soul that is distracted and garrulous. He speaks by His quiet inspirations to a soul that is recollected, to a soul that knows how to keep silence. If silence were strictly observed, there would not be any grumbling, bitterness, slandering, or gossip, and charity would not be tarnished. In a word, many wrongs would not be done. Silent lips are pure gold and bear witness to holiness within. (552)

She also wrote: "The silent soul is capable of attaining the closest union with God. It lives almost always under the inspiration of the Holy Spirit. God works in a silent soul without hindrance" (477).

So our "personal Pentecost" — or more accurately, our series of "personal Pentecosts" — probably doesn't feature driving winds and tongues of fire. More likely, it resembles what the prophet Elijah experienced when the Lord came to him in "a still small voice" (1 Kings 19:12).

A "still small voice"? Less than a whisper, but heard in our hearts. And understood. And on our personal path of conversion, this voice is accepted and acted upon.

A personal prayer. A personal relationship. A personal journey. How? "The Holy Spirit, whose anointing permeates our whole being, is the interior Master of Christian prayer. He is the artisan of the living tradition of prayer. To be sure, there are as many paths of prayer as there are persons who pray, but it is the same Spirit acting in all and with all" (CCC 2672).

Two more bits of encouragement and advice from St. Faustina for all of us:

At the beginning of my religious life, suffering and adversities frightened and disheartened me. So I prayed continuously, asking Jesus to strengthen me and to grant me the power of his Holy Spirit that I might carry out His holy will in all things, because from the beginning I have been aware of my weakness. (56)

Oh, if souls would only be willing to listen, at least a little, to the voice of conscience and the voice — that is, the inspirations — of the Holy Spirit! I say "at least a little," because once we open ourselves to the influence of the Holy Spirit, He himself will fulfill what is lacking in us. (359)

St. Faustina's Prayers

O Spirit of Truth

O Divine Spirit, Spirit of Truth and light,
Dwell ever in my soul by Your divine grace.
May Your breath dissipate the darkness,
And in this light may good deeds be multiplied.

O Divine Spirit, Spirit of love and of mercy,
You pour the balm of trust into my heart,
Your grace confirms my soul in good,
Giving it the invincible power of constancy.

O Divine Spirit, Spirit of peace and of joy,
You invigorate my thirsting heart
And pour into it the living fountain of God's love,
Making it intrepid for battle.

O Divine Spirit, my soul's most welcome guest,
For my part, I want to remain faithful to You;
Both in days of joy and in the agony of suffering,
I want always, O Spirit of God, to live in Your presence.

O Divine Spirit, who pervade my whole being
And give me to know Your Divine, Triune Life,
And lead me into the mystery of Your Divine Being,
Initiating me into Your Divine Essence,
Thus united to You, I will live a life without end. (1411)

O Holy Trinity

O Holy Trinity, in whom is contained the inner life of God, the Father, the Son, and the Holy Spirit, eternal joy, inconceivable depth of love, poured out upon all creatures and constituting their happiness, honor and glory be to Your holy name forever and ever. Amen. (525)

Holy Fear

O Jesus, keep me in the holy fear, so that I may not waste graces. Help me to be faithful to the inspirations of the Holy Spirit. Grant that my heart may burst for love of You, rather than I should neglect even one act of love for You. (1557)

Traditional Prayers to the Holy Spirit

Come, Holy Spirit

Come, Holy Spirit, fill the hearts of Your faithful and enkindle in them the fire of Your love.

V. Send forth Your Spirit and they shall be created.
R. And You shall renew the face of the earth.

Let us pray. O God, who instructed the hearts of the faithful by the light of the Holy Spirit, grant that by that same Spirit we may be truly wise and ever to rejoice in His consolation. Through Christ our Lord. Amen.

Hymn to the Holy Spirit

Come, Holy Spirit, come!
And from your celestial home
*   Shed a ray of light divine!*

Come, Father of the poor!
Come, source of all our store!
*   Come, within our bosoms shine.*

You, of comforters the best;
You, the soul's most welcome guest;
  Sweet refreshment here below;

In our labor, rest most sweet;
Grateful coolness in the heat;
  Solace in the midst of woe.

O most blessed Light divine,
Shine within these hearts of yours,
And our inmost being fill!

Where you are not, we have naught,
Nothing good in deed or thought,
  Nothing free from taint of ill.

Heal our wounds, our strength renew;
On our dryness pour your dew;
  Wash the stains of guilt away.

Bend the stubborn heart and will;
Melt the frozen, warm the chill;
  Guide the steps that go astray.

On the faithful, who adore
And confess you, evermore
  In your sevenfold gift descend;

Give them virtue's sure reward;
Give them your salvation, Lord;
  Give them joys that never end.
  Amen. Alleluia.
(*Lectionary for Mass*, Pentecost Sequence)

Heavenly King, Consoler Spirit

Heavenly King, Consoler Spirit, Spirit of Truth, present everywhere and filling all things, treasure of all good and source of all life, come dwell in us, cleanse and save us, you who are All-Good. (Byzantine Liturgy, Pentecost Vespers, Troparion)

Prayer for the Seven Gifts of the Holy Spirit

Come, Holy Spirit, grant me the gift of wisdom and acceptance so that I may always remember that God's thoughts and God's ways are not often my own.

Come, Holy Spirit, grant me the gift of an understanding heart and mind so that I may always grasp the Infinite Love of God which surpasses everyone and everything.

Come, Holy Spirit, grant me the gift of counsel and courage so that I may always take up my cross and say "Yes" to Jesus in whatever he asks of me.

Come, Holy Spirit, grant me the gift of fortitude and faith so that I may always take courage in Jesus' power and his presence and never be afraid.

Come, Holy Spirit, grant me the gift of knowledge so that I may always know the Truth who is Jesus and his Church's teachings which have set me free.

Come, Holy Spirit, grant me the gift of piety and kindness so that I may always be one who devoutly and loyally serves others in the name of the Holy Trinity.

Come, Holy Spirit, grant me the gift of fear of disappointing the Lord so that I may always honor God in whom I live, and move, and have my being. Amen.

IV. The Power of Intercession

St. Faustina's Mission of Intercession

Jesus charged St. Faustina to intercede for the conversion of sinners. He taught her to pray "unceasingly" the Chaplet of Divine Mercy, which would have great power for the conversion of sinners (687), for great mercy for the dying, and for the eternal salvation of certain souls (1541, 1777).

Faustina devoted herself to intercession every day. "I offered the whole day," she once said, "for dying sinners" (873). She prayed for the women that were cared for by the sisters, and she prayed for the sick, the consecrated religious, her country, and the world.

She also interceded while she worked. For example, while doing needlework, she once prayed, "O Most Holy Trinity dwelling in my heart, I beg You: grant the grace of conversion to as many souls as [the number of] stitches I make today with this crochet hook" (961).

Faustina faithfully interceded for sinners by praying the Rosary, the Chaplet of Divine Mercy, novenas, and litanies. And she also interceded for the lost through her fasting and suffering.

Faustina once demonstrated the power of intercession when she prayed for her younger sister, Wanda. She claimed that her constant prayer "forced God" to grant her sister grace:

> My sister [Wanda] came to see me today. When she told me of her plans, I was horror-stricken. How is such a thing possible? Such a beautiful little soul before the Lord, and yet, great darkness had come over her, and she did not know how to help herself. She had a dark view of everything. The good God entrusted her to my care, and

HOW TO PRAY THE CHAPLET OF DIVINE MERCY

On Rosary beads begin:

Our Father, Hail Mary, the Creed.

On the Our Father beads, pray:

Eternal Father, I offer You the Body and Blood, Soul and Divinity of Your dearly Beloved Son, Our Lord Jesus Christ, in atonement for our sins and those of the whole world.

On the Hail Mary beads, pray:

For the sake of His sorrowful Passion, have mercy on us and on the whole world.

In conclusion, pray three times:

Holy God, Holy Mighty One, Holy Immortal One, have mercy on us and on the whole world.

[Optional conclusion:] Eternal God, in whom mercy is endless and the treasury of compassion inexhaustible, look kindly upon us and increase Your mercy in us, that in difficult moments we might not despair nor become despondent, but with great confidence submit ourselves to Your holy will, which is Love and Mercy itself. (950)

———

St. Faustina wrote:

I realize more and more how much every soul needs God's mercy throughout life and particularly at the hour of death. This chaplet mitigates God's anger, as He Himself told me (1036). "This prayer will serve to appease My wrath" (476).

Its power lies in the reference to the infinite value of the merits of the Passion of Christ (see 367-369).

for two weeks I was able to work with her. But how many sacrifices this soul cost me is known only to God. For no other soul did I bring so many sacrifices and sufferings and prayers before the throne of God as I did for her soul. I felt that I had forced God to grant her grace. When I reflect on all this, I see that it was truly a miracle. Now I can see how much power intercessory prayer has before God. (202)

God wants us to intercede for our loved ones in the same way and "force" Him to grant them the grace they need.

St. Faustina's intercession for the conversion of sinners had extraordinary success. Here she reports remarkable answered prayer for mercy on the world and sinners:

When I immersed myself in prayer and united myself with all the Masses that were being celebrated all over the world at that time, I implored God, for the sake of all these Holy Masses, to have mercy on the world and especially on poor sinners who were dying at that moment. At the same instant, I received an interior answer from God that a thousand souls had received grace through the prayerful mediation I had offered to God. We do not know the number of souls that is ours to save through our prayers and sacrifices; therefore, let us always pray for sinners. (1783)

United with Jesus, let us join St. Faustina to plead for the salvation of souls and for dying sinners. When we pray for the dying, God can give the soul the grace for final repentance. Remember, the dying become the holy souls. We can assist them out of purgatory. They become our powerful intercessors throughout life!

PRAYING WITH ST. FAUSTINA FOR THE LOST

"O Jesus, make my heart sensitive to all the sufferings of my neighbor, whether of body or soul. O my Jesus, I know that You act toward us as we act toward our neighbor." (692)

"O Jesus, eternal Truth, our Life, I call upon You and I beg Your mercy for poor sinners. O sweetest Heart of my Lord, full of pity and unfathomable mercy, I plead with You for poor sinners. O most Sacred Heart, Fount of Mercy from which gush forth rays of inconceivable graces upon the entire human race, I beg of You light for poor sinners. O Jesus, be mindful of Your own bitter Passion and do not permit the loss of souls redeemed at so dear a price of Your most precious Blood." (72)

"Jesus, I beg You, by the inconceivable power of Your mercy, that all the souls who will die today escape the fire of hell, even if they have been the greatest sinners." (873)

Perseverance in Prayer

Jesus taught St. Faustina the importance of persevering in praying for the conversion of sinners. Consider and apply this series of His directives and Faustina's reflections to your practice of intercession:

- Jesus said, "Pray for souls that they be not afraid to approach the tribunal of My mercy. Do not grow weary of praying for sinners. You know what a burden their souls are to My Heart. Relieve My deathly sorrow; dispense My mercy." (975)

- Jesus gave me to understand how a soul should be faithful to prayer despite torments, dryness, and temptations; because oftentimes the realization of God's great plans depends mainly on such prayer. If we do not persevere in such prayer, we frustrate what the Lord wanted to do through us or within us. (872)

- Let the soul be aware that, in order to pray and persevere in prayer, one must arm itself with patience and cope bravely with exterior and interior difficulties. The interior difficulties are discouragement, dryness, heaviness of spirit and temptations. The exterior difficulties are human respect and time; one must observe the time set apart for prayer. (147)

- There are times in life when a soul is in such a state that it does not seem to understand human speech. Everything tires it, and nothing but ardent prayer will put it at ease. In fervent prayer the soul finds relief and, even if it wanted explanations from creatures, these would only make it more restless. (1387)

- Let every soul remember these words: *"And being in anguish, He prayed longer."* I always prolong such prayer as much as is in my power.... (872)

- In the midst of the worst difficulties and adversities, I do not lose inner peace or exterior balance, and this discourages my adversaries. Patience in adversity gives power to the soul. (607)

Jesus never gave up on praying for sinners, but prayed longer! Never give up. We may not see the results in our lifetime, but the grace is there for those we love.

Let's join with Faustina and pray:

Dear God, give me the strength to bear my crosses patiently and to offer up my sufferings in union with my Crucified Savior and His Mother, Our Lady of Sorrows. Help me do this for Your glory and the salvation of souls. Accept my actions as prayers in reparation for my sins and the sins of others, for the needs of this troubled world, and for the holy souls in purgatory. Amen.

ST. FAUSTINA'S PRAYER FOR CONSTANT VIGILANCE

"My Jesus, despite Your graces, I see and feel all my misery. I begin my day with battle and end it with battle. As soon as I conquer one obstacle, ten more appear to take its place. But I am not worried, because I know that this is the time of struggle, not peace. When the burden of the battle becomes too much for me, I throw myself like a child into the arms of the heavenly Father and trust I will not perish. O my Jesus, how prone I am to evil, and this forces me to be constantly vigilant. But I do not lose heart. I trust God's grace, which abounds in the worst misery." (606)

The Power of Intercessory Suffering

Jesus told St. Faustina that her purpose was to become united with Him through love so as to reconcile earth with heaven. He said to her:

I have need of your sufferings to rescue souls. (1612) There is but one price at which souls are bought, and that is suffering united to my suffering on the cross. (324) You will join prayers, fasts, mortifications, labors, and all sufferings to My prayer, fasting, mortification, labors and sufferings and then they will have power before My Father. (531) Help me, My daughter, to save souls. Join your sufferings to My Passion and offer them to the Heavenly Father for sinners. (1032)

So St. Faustina acknowledged the effectiveness of joining her penitential works and suffering with prayer as a means of bringing sinners to conversion. She said: "I saw that my suffering and prayer shackled Satan and snatched many souls from his clutches" (1465). "My sacrifice is nothing in itself, but when I join it to the sacrifice of Jesus Christ, it becomes all-powerful and has the power to appease divine wrath" (482).

And St. Faustina believed that love magnified the power of our intercessory suffering. She said: "Jesus, You have given me to know and understand in what a soul's greatness consists: not in great deeds, but in great love. Love has its worth, and it confers greatness on all our deeds. Although our actions are small and ordinary in themselves, because of love they become great and powerful before God" (889). "The quintessence of love is sacrifice and suffering" (1103).

St. Faustina united herself with Jesus in atonement for sinners. In the events of our lives, we, too, can offer our sufferings and trials for sinners, a truly powerful form of prayer.

———

Today, dear Lord, accept my heartaches and my hardships, my anxiety and my pain, as living, wordless prayers for those who have turned their backs on You, those who have drifted from You, and those who have never heard of or known Your love. Amen.

PART TWO
Praying for Conversion

V. St. Faustina's Prayers for the Conversion of Sinners

Transform Me, O Jesus

Transform me into Yourself, O Jesus, that I may be a living sacrifice and pleasing to You. I desire to atone at each moment for poor sinners. The sacrifice of my spirit is hidden under the veil of the body; the human eye does not perceive it, and for that reason it is pure and pleasing to You. O my Creator and Father of great mercy, I trust in You, for You are Goodness Itself. Souls, do not be afraid of God, but trust in Him, for He is good, and His mercy is everlasting. (908)

O Jesus, how sorry I feel for poor sinners. Jesus, grant them contrition and repentance. Remember Your own sorrowful Passion. I know Your infinite mercy and cannot bear it that a soul that has cost You so much should perish. Jesus, give me the souls of sinners; let Your mercy rest upon them. Take everything away from me, but give me souls. I want to become a sacrificial host for sinners. (908)

Adoration Amid Adversity

Although it is not easy to live in constant agony,
To be nailed to the cross of various pains,
Still, I am inflamed with love by loving,
And like a Seraph I love God, though I am but weakness.

Oh, great is the soul that, midst suffering,
Stands faithfully by God and does His will

And remains uncomforted midst great rainbows and storms,
For God's pure love sweetens her fate.

It is no great thing to love God in prosperity
And thank Him when all goes well,
But rather to adore Him midst great adversities
And love Him for His own sake and place one's hope in Him.

When the soul is in the shadows of Gethsemane,
All alone in the bitterness of pain,
It ascends toward the heights of Jesus,
And though ever drinking bitterness — it is not sad.

When the soul does the will of the Most High God,
Even amidst constant pain and torments,
Having pressed its lips to the chalice proffered,
It becomes mighty, and nothing will daunt it.

Though tortured, it repeats: Your will be done,
Patiently awaiting the moment of its transfiguration,
For, though in deepest darkness, it hears the voice of Jesus: You are
    Mine,
And this it will know fully when the veil falls. (995)

God and Souls: An Act of Oblation

Before heaven and earth, before all the choirs of Angels, before the
Most Holy Virgin Mary, before all the Powers of heaven, I declare
to the One Triune God that today, in union with Jesus Christ, Redeemer of souls, I make a voluntary offering of myself for the conversion of sinners, especially for those souls who have lost hope in
God's mercy. This offering consists in my accepting, with total sub-

jection to God's will, all the sufferings, fears and terrors with which sinners are filled. In return, I give them all the consolations which my soul receives from my communion with God. In a word, I offer everything for them: Holy Masses, Holy Communions, penances, mortifications, prayers.

I do not fear the blows, blows of divine justice, because I am united with Jesus. O my God, in this way I want to make amends to You for the souls that do not trust in Your goodness. I hope against all hope in the ocean of Your mercy. My Lord and my God, my portion — my portion forever, I do not base this act of oblation on my own strength, but on the strength that flows from the merits of Jesus Christ. I will daily repeat this act of self-oblation by pronouncing the following prayer which You Yourself have taught me, Jesus:

"O Blood and Water which gushed forth from the Heart of Jesus as a Fount of Mercy for us, I trust in You!" (309)

Spiritual Communion for Sinners

Before the vigil supper, I entered the chapel for a moment to break the wafer spiritually with those dear to my heart. I presented them all, by name, to Jesus and begged for graces on their behalf. But that wasn't all. I commended to the Lord all those who are being persecuted, those who are suffering, those who do not know His Name, and especially poor sinners. (845)

O Blessed Host, in whom is contained the testament of God's mercy for us, and especially for poor sinners.

O Blessed Host, in whom is contained the Body and Blood of the Lord Jesus as proof of infinite mercy for us, and especially for poor sinners.

O Blessed Host, in whom is contained life eternal and of infinite mercy, dispensed in abundance to us and especially to poor sinners.

O Blessed Host, in whom is contained the mercy of the Father, the Son, and the Holy Spirit toward us, and especially toward poor sinners.

O Blessed Host, in whom is contained the infinite price of mercy which will compensate for all our debts, and especially those of poor sinners.

O Blessed Host, in whom is contained the fountain of living water which springs from infinite mercy for us, and especially for poor sinners.

O Blessed Host, in whom is contained the fire of purest love which blazes forth from the bosom of the Eternal Father, as from an abyss of infinite mercy for us, and especially for poor sinners.

O Blessed Host, in whom is contained the medicine for all our infirmities, flowing from infinite mercy, as from a fount, for us and especially for poor sinners.

O Blessed Host, in whom is contained the union between God and us through His infinite mercy for us, and especially for poor sinners.

O Blessed Host, in whom are contained all the sentiments of the most sweet Heart of Jesus toward us, and especially poor sinners. (356)

Once while saying the Rosary, St. Faustina suddenly saw a ciborium with the Blessed Sacrament, uncovered and full of hosts. She heard a voice from the ciborium saying: "These hosts have been received by souls converted through your prayer and suffering."

VI. Prayers for Mercy on All Mankind

O Greatly merciful God, Infinite Goodness, today all mankind calls out from the abyss of its misery to Your mercy — to Your compassion, O God; and it is with its mighty voice of misery that it cries out. Gracious God, do not reject the prayer of this earth's exiles! (1570)

Prayer for the Salvation of the World

Father, hear our prayers for the salvation of the world. Grant mercy to all souls that turned away from You. Open their hearts and minds with Your light. Gather Your children from the east and the west, from the north and the south. Have mercy, O God, on those who do not know You. Bring them out of darkness into your light.

You are our saving God Who leads us in our salvation. Protect us from evil. Bless and praise You, O Lord, hear our prayers and answer us. You, our Savior, are the hope of all the ends of the earth and the distant seas. May Your way be known upon Earth; among all nations Your salvation. We put the world in Your hands; fill us with Your love. Grant us peace through Christ, Our Lord. Amen.

"God, You did not destroy man after his fall, but in Your mercy You forgave him, You forgave in a divine way; that is, not only have You absolved him from guilt, but You have bestowed upon him every grace. Mercy has moved You to deign to descend among us and lift us up from our misery." (1745)

Novena for the Conversion of All Peoples and Nations

In each of our lives, the conversion of the world begins with our ongoing conversion. Each day we can include in our prayers the men, women, and children who face so many obstacles to their health, safety, and salvation.

For nine days pray the following for each day's intention:

Come, Holy Spirit, and make your home in the hearts of all people throughout the world. Deliver them from sin and suffering. Give them the grace to seek and to find You, the Father, and the Son.

> "With my heart I encompass the whole world, especially countries which are uncivilized or where there is persecution. I am praying for mercy upon them." (742)

Mary, Mother of God and Mother of the Church, pray for us. Amen.

Our Father, Hail Mary, Glory Be.

- **Day One:** For the poor and the marginalized.

- **Day Two:** For the elderly.

- **Day Three:** For those being persecuted or discriminated against because of their faith.

- **Day Four:** For women, that in every country of the world they may be heard and respected.

- **Day Five:** For indigenous people, whose identity and very existence are threatened.

- **Day Six:** For the conversion of the most powerful, and that governments foster greater protection of creation and just distribution of natural resources.

- **Day Seven:** For refugees and for the countries accepting them.

- **Day Eight:** For those who have been, or are being, brutalized by war.

- **Day Nine:** For victimized children of abandonment or violence.

O my God, how I pity those people who do not believe in eternal life; how I pray for them that a ray of mercy would envelop them too, and that God would clasp them to His fatherly bosom. (780)

For Those Who Do Not Yet Know the Love of the Father

As God has made us sharers in His mercy and even more than that, dispensers of that mercy, we should therefore have great love for each soul, beginning with the elect and ending with the soul that does not yet know God. (539)

In the Name of Jesus who said that anything we ask in his Name will be given to those who believe, I ask that those who have not come to know the love of the Heavenly Father will be blessed with the knowledge that they are loved by Him beyond all human reasoning and understanding.

Please grant them the gift to feel His love as it enfolds them to such an extent that they will be unable to resist or deny it. May the knowledge of the Heavenly Father's infinite love stir within their hearts the desire to return that love to Him, and to reflect it to all others. May their lives be a pure reflection of His resplendent love.

I ask this in the Name of the Father, and the Son, and the Holy Spirit, through the Immaculate Heart of Mary. Amen.

A Prayer to the Holy Souls in Purgatory

O holy souls, suffering because you're not yet able to enjoy the vision of God's beauty, I'm truly devoted to you, and I pledge to never forget you and to pray to the Most High for your purification.

O holy souls, assured of salvation as you continue to grow closer to the Blessed Trinity, intercede on my behalf that I can better avoid all dangers to my own eternal salvation.

O holy souls, when life's difficulties are overwhelming me, help me find peace. I ask this not just for myself but for my family and friends. I ask it, too, for those who have hurt me in any way.

O holy souls, be with me as my life on earth ends, and comfort those who mourn my passing. Amen.

VII. Prayers to Our Lady for Conversions

"Then I saw the souls who were doing penance in purgatory.
They appeared like shadows.... I kept praying the
Rosary all the while." (412)
— St. Faustina

A Rosary for Personal Conversion

In 1214, Our Lady appeared to St. Dominic and said the remedy for the world's woes is the Rosary. She taught him that if the Rosary is prayed fervently, then it will bear great fruit, with many graces for souls and many conversions — and that with it will come many saints. Our Lady also said to offer sacrifices, do penance, and pray the Rosary for the salvation of souls! The Rosary is one of the most powerful ways of relieving the souls in purgatory because of the indulgences attached to it.

In Mary's apparitions of Fátima, Lourdes, Beauraing, and Banneux, the message is a call of personal conversion, prayer, and charity. A rosary hung from her arm in all four apparitions, reconfirming that the Rosary is a key devotion for conversion.

Sister Lucia of Fátima was asked when world peace would be restored. She answered: "When a sufficient number of people respond to the Blessed Virgin Mary's call to pray the Rosary and to offer sacrifices for the conversion of sinners."

September 1, 1937. I saw the Lord Jesus, like a king in great majesty, looking down upon our earth with great severity; but because of his Mother's intercession He prolonged the time of His mercy. (1261)

Mary, Immaculate Virgin, take me under Your special protection and guard the purity of my soul, heart, and body. You are the model and star of my life. (874)

———

Mary, you are full of grace! Give us the grace of conversion.

The Joyful Mysteries

1. The Annunciation of the Angel Gabriel to Mary

Dear Jesus, turn my heart away from a narrow, selfish, or selective view of human life. Heavenly Father, I pray now for those suffering, at risk, or facing death because others consider them less than human. Holy Spirit, help me protect all human life, as You are calling me to do.

2. The Visitation of Mary to Elizabeth

Dear Jesus, turn my heart away from the temptation to put myself and my wants first. Heavenly Father, I pray now for those who are friendless, lonely, or feel unloved. Holy Spirit, help me reach out in love, as You are calling me to do.

3. The Nativity of Jesus in Bethlehem

Dear Jesus, turn my heart away from an attitude that makes no room for others. Heavenly Father, I pray now for families facing hunger and homelessness. Holy Spirit, help me be generous to those in need, as You are calling me to be.

4. The Presentation of Jesus in the Temple

Dear Jesus, turn my heart so that, like Simeon and Anna, I never stop looking for You with a patient faith. Heavenly Father, I pray now for the oldest and youngest generations. Holy Spirit, help me encourage and cherish the elders and the little ones in my family, my parish, and my community, as You are calling me to do.

5. The Finding of Jesus in the Temple

Dear Jesus, turn my heart so that I don't lose sight of the fact I, too, am called to be about Your Father's business. Heavenly Father, I pray now for those who don't know You or refuse to believe in You. Holy Spirit, help me be a better disciple and example of the Christian You are calling me to be.

The Luminous Mysteries

1. The Baptism of Jesus in the River Jordan

Dear Jesus, turn my heart so that I can better appreciate and live the graces I received at my baptism. Heavenly Father, I pray now for those who aren't treated as Your beloved son or daughter. Holy Spirit, help me be more welcoming to the newly baptized and those preparing for baptism, as You are calling me to be.

2. The Wedding Feast at Cana

Dear Jesus, turn my heart so that I pay closer attention when Mary whispers to me: "Do whatever He tells you." Heavenly Father, I pray now for those whose marriage is troubled. Holy Spirit, help me play the part You're calling me to play in being a "miracle" that helps others.

3. The Proclamation of the Kingdom of God

Dear Jesus, turn my heart so that every day I answer Your call to personal conversion. Heavenly Father, I pray now for those who have yet to truly hear what

Your Son is offering them. Holy Spirit, help me proclaim God's kingdom to those around me, in my actions and my choices, as You are calling me to do.

4. The Transfiguration of Jesus

Dear Jesus, turn my heart and transform my soul. Heavenly Father, I pray now for those whose lives and souls are being damaged by sin. Holy Spirit, help me be the light to the world You are calling me to be.

5. The Institution of the Eucharist

Dear Jesus, turn my heart closer to You each time I receive Your precious Body and Blood. Heavenly Father, I pray now for those who are unable to receive the Eucharist. Holy Spirit, help me share Christ's love with others, as You are calling me to do.

The Sorrowful Mysteries

1. The Agony in the Garden

Dear Jesus, turn my heart so that, no matter what I'm facing, I have the courage and faith to say, "Thy will be done." Heavenly Father, I pray now for those who are nearing death and for those who love them. Holy Spirit, help me not run or hide from those who are in pain but offer them the support You are calling me to offer.

2. The Scourging at the Pillar

Dear Jesus, turn my heart so that I willingly accept the hurtful or harsh consequences of following You. Heavenly Father, I pray now for those are incarcerated and for their families. Holy Spirit, as You are calling me to do, help me remember to pray for the martyrs of today.

3. The Crowning with Thorns

Dear Jesus, turn my heart so that my life isn't a mockery of my professed belief in You. Heavenly Father, I pray now for those who look for complete fulfillment in the crowns the world has to offer. Holy Spirit, help me answer Your call to be quick to offer praise and encouragement to those who receive little or none of either.

4. The Carrying of the Cross

Dear Jesus, turn my heart so that sin, fear, or apathy doesn't get in the way of my taking up my crosses daily. Heavenly Father, I pray now for those whose burdens are so overwhelming. Holy Spirit, help me be a voluntary "Simon of Cyrene" to those carrying a heavy cross, as You are asking me to be.

5. The Crucifixion

Dear Jesus, turn my heart so that I never fail to see and remember what You have done for me. Heavenly Father, I pray now for those who are grieving the death of a loved one. Holy Spirit, help me die to sin and self-centeredness and choose to live the life of love You are offering me to live.

The Glorious Mysteries

1. The Resurrection

Dear Jesus, turn my heart so that I rise each day eager to follow You more closely. Heavenly Father, I pray now for those who don't know of Your mercy and so are very afraid of dying. Holy Spirit, help me be the "Easter person" — someone who believes in the resurrection of the body and life everlasting — You are calling me to be.

2. The Ascension

Dear Jesus, turn my heart and lift my gaze to "see" You in Your heavenly glory. Heavenly Father, I pray now for those who believe there is no God or are unsure of Your existence. Holy Spirit, even when it feels as if Jesus has left me, help me remain the strong and faithful follower You are calling me to be.

3. The Descent of the Holy Spirit

Dear Jesus, turn my heart so that I better receive the Holy Spirit in my own life, in my own mind, and in my own soul. Heavenly Father, I pray now for those who actively and viciously work to wipe out the Holy Spirit-led Church. Holy Spirit, help me pay attention to the gifts, the fruits — and the nudges — You give me, and to use them all to serve God and others.

4. The Assumption of Mary

Dear Jesus, turn my heart so that I better follow the example set by Your Blessed Mother. Heavenly Father, I pray now for those unable or unwilling to see the spiritual, and the miraculous, in our world. Holy Spirit, help me answer Your invitation to get to know Our Lady better and to love her more.

5. The Coronation of Mary

Dear Jesus, turn my heart so that I can better honor my Queen. Heavenly Father, I pray now for those who abuse their civil, political, or military authority. Holy Spirit, help me live the life You ask me to live, as one who is part of a truly royal family that includes Christ the King and the Queen of Heaven.

Responding to Mary's Call for Conversion

To Our Lady of Fátima

Queen of the Rosary, sweet Virgin of Fátima, who has deigned to appear in the land of Portugal and has brought peace, both interior and exterior, to that once so troubled country, we beg of you to watch over our own dear homeland and to assure its moral and spiritual revival.

Bring back peace to all nations of the world, so that all, and our own nation in particular, may be happy to call you their Queen and the Queen of Peace.

Our Lady of the Rosary, pray for our country. Our Lady of Fátima, obtain for all humanity a durable peace. Amen.

Prayer to Our Lady of the Atonement

We salute you, Holy Mary,
Daughter of the Father,
and entreat you to obtain for us
a devotion like your own to the most Sweet Will of God.

We salute you,
Virgin Mother of God the Son,
and entreat you to obtain for us
such union with the Sacred Heart of Jesus
that our own hearts may burn with love of God
and an ardent zeal for the salvation of souls.

We salute you,
Immaculate Spouse of God the Holy Spirit,
and entreat you to obtain for us
such yielding of ourselves to the Blessed Spirit

that He may, in all things,
direct and rule our hearts
and that we may never grieve Him
in thought, word, or deed. Amen.

Obedient to the Invitation
(Prayer of Pope Pius XII to Our Lady of Lourdes)

Obedient to the invitation given in your own maternal words,
O Virgin Immaculate of Lourdes,
we hurry to your feet at the humble grotto,
where you appeared to point out the way of prayer
and penance to those gone astray
and to dispense the graces and wonders
of your supreme goodness to the sick.

O gracious Queen,
accept the homage and the prayers
that the peoples and the nations,
caught in bitter straits,
trustingly raise to you.

O resplendent vision of Paradise,
dispel from our minds the darkness of error
by the light of faith!
O mystical garden of roses,
comfort the broken hearts of people
with the heavenly perfume of hope!
O inexhaustible fountain of saving waters,
refresh with the floods of divine charity
the hearts that are dry.

Grant that we, your children,
may be consoled in our sorrows,
protected in danger,
and sustained in our struggles!
May we love and serve your dear Son Jesus in such a way
that we may deserve eternal joy
before your throne in heaven above. Amen.

Novena Prayer to Our Lady of Beauraing

On November 29, 1932, Mary appeared to five children in the small town of Beauraing in Belgium. She stated, "I will convert sinners. I am the Mother of God, Queen of Heaven." She called for prayer for the conversion of sinners. She revealed her Golden Heart and asked us to sacrifice for her.

———

Our Lady of Beauraing, Immaculate Virgin, carry to Jesus, your Son, all the intentions which we confide to you this day. (Mention your intentions.)

Mother with the Golden Heart, mirror of the tenderness of the Father, look with love upon the men and women of our time and fill them with the joy of your presence.

You who promised to convert sinners, help us discover the infinite mercy of our God. Awaken in us the grace of conversion so that all our life becomes the reflection of this mercy.

Holy Mother of God, look down upon our miseries, console us in our sorrows, give strength to all those who are suffering.

Queen of Heaven, crowned with light, help us to grow in faith, hope, and love, and we shall be able to give thanks without end.

You brought Jesus into the world, may we by prayer, by sharing His Word, and by testimony of our life filled with love and joy make Him be born in all hearts.

May every instant of our life be a YES to the question, which you are asking us today: Do you love my Son? Do you love me? Then the reign of Jesus will come into the world.

Prayer to Our Lady of Banneux

Twelve days after Our Lady appeared in Beauraing, she made her presence known again in Banneux as "Our Lady of the Poor."

———

Our Lady of Banneux, Virgin of the Poor, you have said: "I come to relieve suffering." Holy Mother of God and Mother of the Savior, you make us hear anew the merciful call of your divine Son: "Come to me, all you who are burdened and who suffer, and I will relieve you." Mother of all men, you have come for all nations and you ask us to pray much. We place our trust in you. Deign to hear our prayers. Look upon our spiritual and temporal miseries. Lead back to Jesus the poor straying souls and increase the faith of the faithful. Holy Virgin Mary, bring aid to the indigent; help us to sanctify the trials of life; relieve the sick and pray for all your children. O Virgin of the Poor, you are our hope! By your maternal mediation, may the reign of Christ the King spread over all nations. Amen.

Mother of Good Counsel

Mary, I renounce my spirit,
And I ask for your spirit.
Mary, take away my thoughts,
And given me your thoughts.
Mary, take away my desires,

And give me your desires.
Mary take away my feelings,
And give me your feelings.

I am totally yours,
And everything I have I offer You,
O my beloved Jesus, through Mary
Your most Holy Mother.

Come, Holy Spirit, come by
Means of the powerful intercession of the
Immaculate Heart of Mary,
Your well-beloved spouse.

Hail Mary.... Mother of Good Counsel, give us good counsel. Amen. (Three times.)

Prayer to Our Lady of Siluva for Coming Back to the Faith

In the early seventeenth century, a reported apparition of Mary in Siluva, Lithuania, led many of the townspeople to return to the practice of the Faith.

O most holy Virgin Mary, who has appeared
at various times in history and to diverse peoples,
we remember now especially your tears at Siluva
and your sad voice saying, "You plow and plant
seed here where formerly my Son was honored."
May we be moved as those ancients were,
And so work to revive within our hearts
a spirit of adoration for your Son.

*Strengthen the weak structures of our families and grant
that our hearts may welcome your presence.
Teach us to seek forgiveness for our sins,
and for the sins of our nation and of the Church.*

*O Mother of God, we desire to raise up the glory
of your revelation from forgotten ruins that we may
all the more honor you as our patroness and,
with your help, obtain the spirit of a living faith.
Through Christ Our Lord. Amen.*

A Solemn Act of Consecration to the Immaculate Heart of Mary
(Prayer of Pope Pius XII)

Most Holy Virgin Mary, tender Mother of men, to fulfill the desires of the Sacred Heart of Jesus and the request of the Vicar of your Son on earth, we consecrate ourselves and our families to your Sorrowful and Immaculate Heart, O Queen of the Most Holy Rosary, and we recommend to you all the people of our country and all the world. Please accept our consecration, dearest Mother, and use us as you wish to accomplish your designs in the world.

O Sorrowful and Immaculate Heart of Mary, Queen of the Most Holy Rosary, and Queen of the World, rule over us, together with the Sacred Heart of Jesus Christ, Our King. Save us from the spreading flood of modern paganism; kindle in our hearts and homes the love of purity, the practice of a virtuous life, an ardent zeal for souls, and a desire to pray the Rosary more faithfully.

We come with confidence to you, O Throne of Grace and Mother of Fair Love. Inflame us with the same Divine Fire which has inflamed your own Sorrowful and Immaculate Heart. Make our hearts and homes your shrine, and through us, make the Heart of Jesus, together with your rule, triumph in every heart and home. Amen.

O Sweet Mother

O sweet Mother of God,
I model my life on You;
You are for me the bright dawn;
In You I lose myself, enraptured.

O Mother, Immaculate Virgin,
In You the divine ray is reflected,
Midst storms, 'tis You who teach me to love the Lord,
O my shield and defense from the foe. (1232)

VIII. Prayers for Transformation in Christ

Litany of the Saints for Growth in Holiness

The saints model conversion for us. All of them turned away from sin and turned to God. Consider the lives of St. Francis of Assisi and St. Ignatius of Loyola. Neither had a Damascus Road experience like St. Paul. Each was converted to Christ over a series of years and continued to grow in holiness lifelong. St. Thérèse of Lisieux had to struggle with scruples and fear on her road to sainthood. While St. Paul enjoyed a dramatic initial conversion, his transformation took a lifetime.

THE SECRET OF SANCTITY

St. Faustina recorded her conversion and transformation in her *Diary*. And she explained the secret that led her and all the saints to holiness: "There is one word I heed and continually ponder; it alone is everything to me; I live by it and die by it, and it is the holy will of God. It is my daily food. My whole soul listens intently to God's wishes. I do always what God asks of me, although my nature often quakes and I feel that the magnitude of these things is beyond my strength. I know well what I am of myself, but I also know what the grace of God is, which supports me." (652)

February 10, 1938. During meditation, the Lord gave me knowledge of the joy of heaven and of the saints on our arrival there; they love

God as the sole object of their love, but they also have a tender and heartfelt love for us. It is from the face of God that this joy flows out upon all, because we see Him face to face. His face is so sweet that the soul falls anew into ecstasy. (1592)

Pray this litany to ask for the intercession of St. Faustina and the saints for the graces you need to become a saint by being faithful to the inspirations of the Holy Spirit.

———

Lord, have mercy.
Christ, have mercy.
Lord, have mercy.

> *St. Paul, preserve me from human pride and lead me to embrace Christ crucified.*
> *St. Margaret of Cortona, preserve me from despair and lead me to be a peacemaker.*
> *Bl. Angela of Foligno, preserve me from gossiping and lead me to think good of all.*
> *St. John of God, preserve me from strange behavior and lead me to help the poor.*
> *St. Dismas, preserve me from thievery and lead me to give myself over to Jesus.*
> *St. Mary of Egypt, preserve me from phoniness and lead me to be honest with others.*
> *Bl. Giles of Portugal, preserve me from yielding to Satan and lead me to Divine Truth.*
> *Ven. Matt Talbot, preserve me from addictions and lead me to a truly balanced life.*

St. Camillus de Lellis, preserve me from self-pity and lead me to assist the sick.

St. Mary Magdalen, preserve me from anxiety and lead me to proclaim the Risen Christ.

St. Olaf the Viking, preserve me from violence and lead me to forgive my enemies.

St. Ignatius of Loyola, preserve me from doubts and lead me to discern what is right.

St. Augustine, preserve me from sensuality and lead me to rest my desires in God.

St. Peter Claver, preserve me from timidity and lead me to assist the oppressed.

St. Matthew, preserve me from dishonesty and lead me to share with others.

St. Thérèse of Lisieux, preserve me from petty irritations and lead me to the way of love.

St. Francis of Assisi, preserve me from love of wealth and lead me to humble poverty.

St. Faustina, preserve me from being misunderstood and lead me to Jesus, Divine Mercy.

St. Pelagia the Penitent, preserve me from promiscuity and lead me to a chaste life.

Pope St. Callistus I, preserve me from prejudice and lead me to acceptance of others.

St. Fabiola the Bigamist, preserve me from infidelity and lead me to correct my actions.

St. Thomas Becket, preserve me from worldly concerns and lead me to practice the Faith.

Lamb of God, who takes away the sins of the world — spare us, O Lord.
Lamb of God, who takes away the sins of the world — graciously hear us, O Lord.
Lamb of God, who takes away the sins of the world — have mercy on us.

Our Father, Hail Mary, Glory Be.

BE A SAINT

"Let no soul, even the most miserable, fall prey to doubt; for, as long as one is alive, each one can become a great saint, so great is the power of God's grace. It remains only for us not to oppose God's action." (283)

"When you unite Yourself with me in Communion, O God,
I then feel my unspeakable greatness,
A greatness which flows from You, O Lord, I humbly confess,
And despite my misery, with Your help, I can become a saint."
(1718)

The Beatitudes of Conversion

Whatever Jesus did, He did well. He went along, doing good. His manner was full of goodness and mercy. His steps were guided by compassion. Toward His enemies He showed goodness, kindness, and understanding, and to those in need help and consolation. (1175)

The Beatitudes (Mt 5:3-10) enable conversion experiences. They are guideposts for righteous living that describe behaviors leading us to holiness. "The Beatitudes," says the *Catechism*, "confront us with decisive choices concerning earthly goods; they purify our hearts in order to teach us to love God above all things" (n. 1728).

St. Faustina meditated on the Beatitudes and believed that by conforming to them we would enjoy their benefits. She said, "... I received an inner understanding of the great reward that God is preparing for us, not only for our good deeds, but also for our sincere desire to perform them. What a great grace of God this is!" (450).

Living the Beatitudes is one of the central ways to avoid purgatory.

"Blessed are the poor in spirit, for theirs is the kingdom of heaven."

- Do I sacrifice for others?
- Can I admit mistakes without blaming others?
- Have I been selfish, self-centered, greedy, or possessive?
- Do I contribute my time, talent, and money to the poor?

———

Jesus, Supreme Light, grant me the grace of knowing myself, and pierce my dark soul with Your Light, and fill the abyss of my soul with Your own self.... (297)

"Blessed are those who mourn, for they shall be comforted."

- Do I console those who mourn and suffer?
- Do I have compassion for the poor, the hungry, and the addicted; the sick, the lonely, and the sinful?
- Have I been able to say "I'm sorry" and mean it?
- Do I endure difficulties and afflictions with faith and patience?

———

Jesus, make my heart like unto Yours, or rather transform it into Your own Heart that I may sense the needs of other hearts, especially those who are sad and suffering. May the rays of mercy rest in my heart. (514)

"Blessed are the meek, for they shall inherit the earth."

- Am I authentically humble and self-giving?
- Do I respect the worth of others?
- Am I a good listener?
- Have I been impatient, resentful, bitter, unforgiving, or insulting and abusive to others?
- Do I manipulate or dominate others?
- Have I lost my temper?

———

Help me, O Lord, that my heart may be merciful so that I myself may feel all the sufferings of my neighbor. I will refuse my heart to no one. I will be sincere even with those who, I know, will abuse my kindness. (163)

"Blessed are those who hunger and thirst for righteousness, for they shall be satisfied."

- Am I passionate for the things of God?
- Am I able to suffer in silence, or am I always complaining about something?
- Have I prayed for my enemies?
- Have I failed to defend someone for fear of humiliation or persecution?
- Have I the courage to stand up for the truth despite criticism, ridicule, or persecution?
- Am I afraid to witness my faith?

Mother of God, Your soul was plunged into a sea of bitterness; look upon Your child and teach her to suffer and to love while suffering. Fortify my soul that pain will not break it. Mother of grace, teach me to live by [the power of] God. (315)

"Blessed are the merciful, for they shall obtain mercy."

- Am I sensitive to others' needs?
- Am I forgiving and merciful?
- Do I give others the benefit of the doubt? Am I harsh and judgmental?
- Do I expect mercy but do not want to grant it?
- Do I give to others without wanting in return?
- Whom have I turned my back on who was poor, hungry, rejected, lonely, or needy?

"Jesus, I beg You, by the inconceivable power of Your mercy, that all souls who will die today escape the fire of hell, even if they have been the greatest sinners…. [B]ecause Your mercy is inconceivable, the Angels will not be surprised at this." (873)

"Blessed are the pure in heart, for they shall see God."

- Have I allowed a particular sin or vice to distract me from God?
- Am I trustworthy?
- Do I treat others with respect and love?
- Have I ever used anyone as an object of my own pleasure?
- Have the motives or intentions of my actions been selfish?

- Am I prejudiced?
- Am I a person of sincerity?

———

Mary, Immaculate Virgin, take me under Your special protection and guard the purity of my soul, heart and body. You are the model and star of my life. (874)

"Blessed are the peacemakers, for they shall be called sons of God."

- Do I hold grudges or seek revenge?
- Do I accept those who do not agree with me?
- Am I at peace with myself, my family, and those with whom I work?
- Am I at peace with God?

———

O Jesus, have mercy! Embrace the whole world and press me to Your Heart.... (869)

"Blessed are those who are persecuted for righteousness' sake, for theirs is the kingdom of heaven."

- Am I willing to sacrifice anything for my faith?
- Do I "go along with the crowd" because I fear the consequences of standing up for the truth?
- Do I allow human respect to keep me from being a Christian witness?
- Who are my heroes?
- Do I live confident of the promises of Jesus?

———

O Eternal Truth, support me that I may have the courage to speak the truth even if it would come about that I would pay for it with my life. O Jesus, how hard it is to believe in this, when one sees one thing taught and something else lived. (1482)

St. Faustina's Acts of Faith, Hope, Charity, and Joy

The novices in St. Faustina's community loved to recreate with her. They would call her the "theologian." She often talked to them about the virtues of faith, hope, and charity, and she encouraged them to pray for the holy souls in purgatory.

The souls there exercise perfectly the virtues of faith, hope, charity, and joy, radiating divine goodness and charity. That's why they urge us to learn here on earth what they're learning in purgatory, that of attaining union with, and transformation in, God through love.

Act of Faith

I want to live in the spirit of faith. I accept everything that comes my way as given me by the loving will of God, who sincerely desires my happiness. (1549)

I fervently beg the Lord to strengthen my faith, so that in my drab, everyday life I will not be guided by human dispositions, but by those of the spirit. Oh, how everything drags man towards the earth! But lively faith maintains the soul in the highest regions and assigns self-love its proper place; that is to say, the lowest one. (210)

Act of Hope

O my Jesus, my Master and Director, strengthen and enlighten me in these difficult moments of my life. I expect no help from people; all my hope is in You. I feel alone in the face of Your demands, O Lord. Despite the fears and qualms of my nature, I am fulfilling Your holy will and desire to fulfill it as faithfully as possible throughout my life and in my death. Jesus, with You I can do all things. Do with me as You please; only give me Your merciful Heart and that is enough for me. (650)

Amid the greatest torments, I fix the gaze of my soul upon Jesus Crucified; I do not expect help from people, but place my trust in God. In His unfathomable mercy lies all my hope. (681)

"I understand souls who are suffering against hope, for I have gone through that fire myself. But God will not give [us anything] beyond our strength. Often have I lived hoping against hope, and have advanced my hope to complete trust in God. Let that which He has ordained from all ages happen to me.... You are the sweet hope for sinful man.... Your most merciful Heart is all my hope.... In You I have the light of hope." (386, 951, 1065, 1321)

Act of Charity

Today a girl came to see me. I saw that she was suffering, but not so much in body as in soul. I comforted her as much as I could, but my words of consolation were not enough. She was a poor orphan with a soul plunged in bitterness and pain. She opened her soul to me and told me everything. I understood that, in this case, simple words of consolation would not be enough. I fervently interceded with the Lord for that soul and offered Him my joy so that He would give it to her and take all feeling of joy away from me. And the Lord heard

"TO THE LEAST OF MY BROTHERS …"

"Jesus came to the main entrance today, under the guise of a poor young man. This young man, emaciated, barefoot and bareheaded, and with his clothes in tatters, was frozen because the day was cold and rainy. He asked for something hot to eat. So I went to the kitchen, but found nothing there for the poor. But, after searching around for some time, I succeeded in finding some soup, which I reheated and into which I crumbled some bread, and I gave it to the poor young man, who ate it. As I was taking the bowl from him, he gave me to know that He was the Lord of heaven and earth. When I saw Him as He was, He vanished from my sight. When I went back in and reflected on what had happened at the gate, I heard these words in my soul: My daughter, the blessings of the poor who bless Me as they leave this gate have reached My ears. And your compassion, within the bounds of obedience, has pleased Me, and this is why I came down from My throne — to taste the fruits of your mercy." (1312)

"O my Jesus, now everything is clear to me, and I understand all that has just happened. I somehow felt and asked myself what sort of a poor man is this who radiates such modesty. From that moment on, there was stirred up in my heart an even purer love toward the poor and the needy. Oh, how happy I am that my superiors have given me such a task! I understand that mercy is manifold; one can do good always and everywhere and at all times. An ardent love of God sees all around itself constant opportunities to share itself through deed, word and prayer." (1313)

my prayer: I was left only with the consolation that she had been consoled. (864)

Act of Joy

My soul was flooded with joy beyond understanding, and the Lord gave me to experience the whole ocean and abyss of His fathomless mercy. Oh, if only souls would want to understand how much God loves them! All comparisons, even if they were the most tender and the most vehement, are but a mere shadow when set against the reality. (1073)

O incomprehensible God, my heart dissolves in joy that You have allowed me to penetrate the mysteries of Your mercy! Everything begins with Your mercy and ends with Your mercy. (1506)

IX. Prayers to the Saints for Conversion

To St. Alban, Patron of Converts

Heavenly Father, St. Alban was converted by a priest whom he sheltered from persecutions and rescued by changing clothes with him. As the patron saint of converts, I ask him to pray with me for all the people I know who have not yet converted. O Lord, remove from their lives all the crutches they have been leaning on when they should be turning to You. When people can sink no lower, help them to see that they have nowhere else to turn, so that they look upwards to You and realize it's You they need. Send angels and people into their lives who will deliver them into Your arms. St. Alban, pray for us. Amen.

Prayer to St. Monica

[Jesus said to St. Faustina:] Conversion, as well as perseverance, is a grace of my mercy. (1577)

———

Exemplary Mother of the Great Augustine,
you perseveringly pursued your wayward son
not with threats but with prayerful cries to heaven.
Intercede for all mothers in our day
so that they may learn to draw their children to God.
Teach them how to remain close to their children,
even the prodigal sons and daughters who have sadly gone astray.
Dear St. Monica, troubled wife and mother,
many sorrows pierced your heart during your lifetime.

Yet, you never despaired or lost faith.
With confidence, persistence, and profound faith,
you prayed daily for the conversion
of your beloved husband, Patricius,
and your beloved son, Augustine;
your prayers were answered.
Grant me that same fortitude, patience,
and trust in the Lord.
Intercede for me, dear St. Monica,
that God may favorably hear my plea
(mention your intention here).
Grant me the grace to accept His will in all things,
through Jesus Christ, our Lord,
in the unity of the Holy Spirit,
one God, forever and ever. Amen.

Prayer of St. Augustine for Conversion

God Our Father, You who exhort us to pray to You,
give us what has been asked of You, listen to me,
who am shivering in this darkness, and stretch out
Your hand to me. Let me see Your light. Bring me
back from errors and bring it about that under Your
guidance I may return again to myself and to You.
O God, who consoled the sorrowful
and who mercifully accepted the motherly
tears of St. Monica for the conversion of her son Augustine,
grant us, through the intercession of them both, that we may bitterly
regret our sins and find the grace of Your pardon. Amen.

Litany to St. John the Baptist

St. John the Baptist, the forerunner of the early Desert Fathers and patron of monastic life, lived an austere life of personal sacrifice and baptized large groups of penitents in the Jordan River. "In those days came John the Baptist, preaching in the wilderness of Judea, 'Repent, for the kingdom of heaven is at hand' " (Mt 3:1-2).

Lord, have mercy on us.
Christ, hear us.
God the Son, Redeemer of the world — have mercy on us.
God, the Holy Spirit — have mercy on us.
Holy Trinity, One God — have mercy on us.

Holy Mary — hear our prayer
Queen of prophets ...
Queen of martyrs ...
St. John the Baptist ...
St. John the Baptist, precursor of Christ ...
St. John the Baptist, glorious forerunner of the Sun of Justice ...
St. John the Baptist, minister of baptism to Jesus ...
St. John the Baptist burning and shining lamp to the world ...
St. John the Baptist, angel of purity before your birth ...
St. John the Baptist, special friend and favorite of Christ ...
St. John the Baptist, heavenly contemplative, whose element was
    prayer ...
St. John the Baptist, intrepid preacher of truth ...
St. John the Baptist, voice crying in the wilderness ...
St. John the Baptist, miracle of mortification and penance ...

St. John the Baptist, example of profound humility ...
St. John the Baptist, glorious martyr of zeal for God's holy law ...
St. John the Baptist, gloriously fulfilling your mission ...

Lamb of God, who takes away the sins of the world — spare us, O Lord.
Lamb of God, who takes away the sins of the world — graciously hear us, O Lord.
Lamb of God, who takes away the sins of the world — have mercy on us.

Pray for us, O glorious St. John the Baptist, that we may be worthy of the promises of Christ.

O God, who has honored this world by the birth of St. John the Baptist, grant that your faithful people may rejoice in the way of eternal salvation, through Jesus Christ Our Lord. Amen.

St. Margaret Mary Alacoque's Prayer for Prodigals

Loving heart of Jesus, move hearts that are harder than rock, melt spirits that are colder than ice, reach souls that are more impenetrable than diamonds. Amen.

Prayer to St. Joseph for a Conversion

St. Joseph is among the most venerated saints in St. Faustina's congregation. Statues of him are to be found in every one of their convents.

St. Joseph urged me to have a constant devotion to him. He himself told me to recite three prayers [the Our Father, Hail Mary, and Glory Be] and the *Memorare* once every day.... *[This prayer is said daily by her congregation.]* I recite the requested prayers every day and feel his special protection. (1203)

Oh, glorious patriarch St. Joseph, who merited to be called "just" by the Holy Spirit, I urgently recommend to you the soul of [name], which Jesus redeemed at the price of His precious Blood.

You know how deplorable is the state and how unhappy the life of those who have banished this loving Savior from their hearts, and how greatly they are exposed to the danger of losing Him eternally. Permit not, I beseech you, that a soul so dear to me should continue any longer along evil ways. Preserve it from the danger that threatens it as you touch the heart of this prodigal child and guide him back to Our Lord and all who love Him. Abandon him not, I implore you, till you have opened to him the gates of the heavenly city, where he will praise and bless you throughout eternity for the happiness which he will owe to your powerful intercession. Amen.

Prayer to St. Joseph for Purity

And Jesus gave me to know for what sins He subjected himself to the scourging: these are sins of impurity. (445)

Jesus, lover of chastity, Mary, Mother most pure, and Joseph, chaste Guardian of the Virgin, to you I come at this hour, begging you to plead for me before God. I earnestly wish to be pure in thought, word, and deed in imitation of your own holy purity.

Obtain for me, then, a deep sense of modesty which will be reflected in my external conduct. Protect my eyes, the windows of my soul, from anything that might dim the luster of a heart that must mirror only Christ-like purity.

And when the "Bread of Angels becomes the Bread of me" in my heart at Holy Communion, seal my heart forever against the suggestions of sinful pleasures.

Heart of Jesus, Fount of all purity, have mercy on us.

Prayer to St. Anthony for Conversion

Anthony is not only the patron of finding lost objects, but of finding lost souls!

———

Loving St. Anthony, you always reached out in compassion to those who had lost their faith. You were especially concerned because they had given up access to the healing words of Jesus found in the Sacrament of Reconciliation and in the nourishing presence of Jesus in the Sacrament of the Eucharist.

Intercede for all who have stopped practicing their faith. Reawaken in their hearts a love for our Church and the sacraments, and kindle in their hearts a sense of forgiveness for the ways they might have been hurt by members of the Church who fell short of the teaching of Christ.

Finally, St. Anthony, help me to respond to my own call to conversion so that I might become an example of someone who has found great peace in the arms of Christ. May the joy I experience as a Catholic be an invitation to those who are lost to come home again to the Church which we love. Amen.

Litany of Longing

Lord, have mercy on us.
Christ, have mercy on us.
Lord, have mercy on us.
Christ hear us. Christ, graciously hear us.
God the Father, Creator of the world — have mercy on us.
God the Son, Redeemer of the world — have mercy on us.
God the Holy Spirit, Truth in the world — have mercy on us.
Most Blessed Trinity, One God — have mercy on us!

Holy Mary, Mother of God — Pray *for us.*
Holy Mary, Queen of all angels …
Holy Mary, Queen of all saints …
Holy Mary, Queen of all hearts …

All you angels and saints — *pray for us.*
Poor souls in purgatory …

Struggling souls full of longing — *we pray for you.*
Abandoned children full of longing …
Abandoned youths full of longing …
Abandoned mothers …
Abandoned sick …
Abandoned old and poor …
Abandoned homeless …
Abandoned ones in danger …
Abandoned, straying souls …
Abandoned fallen souls …
Abandoned desperate souls …
Abandoned dying souls …

In our painful longing for You — *help us, merciful God.*
In our painful longing for love …
In our painful longing for understanding …
In our painful longing for peace …
In our painful longing for health …
In our painful longing for our home …
In our painful longing for tranquility of heart …
In our painful longing for the forgiveness of our sins …
In our painful longing to make reparation …

Promise to quench our longing, loving Father in heaven.

Promise to accept our longing as a sacrifice, Crucified Redeemer.

Promise to sanctify our longing, Comforter, Holy Spirit.

Take us firmly by the hand, O holy angels, and do not let any of us be lost.

Place us under your protective mantle, Blessed Mary, Mother of Grace.

Holy God, Holy Mighty One, Holy Immortal One, lead us home to You where all our longing will be eternally fulfilled, healed, and transformed into joy. Amen.

X. Meditations on the Passion with St. Faustina

The Triduum of Conversion

For God so loved the world, he gave his only Son, that whoever believes in him should not perish but have eternal life.
— John 3:16

[Jesus said to St. Faustina:] There is more merit to one hour of meditation on My sorrowful Passion than there is to a whole year of flagellation that draws blood. (369) There are few souls who contemplate My Passion with true feeling; I give great graces to souls who meditate devoutly on My Passion. (737) My daughter, meditate frequently on the sufferings which I have undergone for your sake, and then nothing of what you suffer for Me will seem great to you. You please Me most when you meditate on My Sorrowful Passion. Join your little sufferings to My Sorrowful Passion, so that they may have infinite value before My Majesty. (1512)

"He who wants to learn true humility should reflect upon the Passion of Jesus." (267)

"Today, I felt the Passion of Jesus in my own whole body, and the Lord gave me knowledge of the conversion of certain souls. (1627).... The pain is very great, but all this for the sake of immortal souls." (1010)

Institution of the Eucharist

Holy Hour. — Thursday. During this hour of prayer, Jesus allowed me to enter the Cenacle, and I was a witness to what happened there. However, I was most deeply moved when, before the Consecration, Jesus raised His eyes to heaven and entered into a mysterious conversation with His Father. It is only in eternity that we shall really understand that moment. His eyes were like two flames; His face was radiant, white as snow; His whole personage full of majesty, His soul full of longing. At the moment of Consecration, love rested satiated — the sacrifice fully consummated. Now only the external ceremony of death will be carried out — external destruction; the essence [of it] is in the Cenacle. Never in my whole life had I understood this mystery so profoundly as during that hour of adoration. Oh, how ardently I desire that the whole world would come to know this unfathomable mystery! (684)

Convert me, Jesus, from spiritual hunger, and let me become one with You in the Eucharist.

Jesus in Gethsemane

I spent this whole night with Jesus in the dark dungeon. This was a night of adoration. The sisters were praying in the chapel, and I was uniting myself with them in spirit, because poor health prevents me from going to the chapel. But all night long I could not fall asleep, so I spent the night in the dark prison with Jesus. Jesus gave me to know of the sufferings He experienced there. The world will learn about them on the day of judgment. (1515)

O Divine Will, You are the delight of my heart, the food of my soul, the light of my intellect, the omnipotent strength of my will; for when I unite myself with Your will, O Lord, Your power works through me and takes the place of my feeble will. Each day, I seek to carry out God's wishes. (650)

Convert me, Jesus, from rebelling against God, and let me abandon my will to You.

The Agony

… I took part in His Agony in the Garden, and that He Himself allowed these sufferings in order to offer reparation to God for the souls murdered in the womb. (1276)

From my breast there escaped one continuous moan. A natural dying will be much easier, because then one is in agony and will die; while here, one is in agony, but cannot die. O Jesus, I never thought such suffering could exist. Nothingness: that is the reality. O Jesus, save me! (1558)

Convert me Jesus from refusing to suffer, and let me repair my wrongs against You.

The Scourging

… I saw the Lord Jesus tied to a pillar, stripped of His clothes, and the scourging began immediately.… (445) I saw how the Lord Jesus suffered as He was being scourged. Oh, such an inconceivable agony! … His blood flowed to the ground, and in some places His flesh started to fall off. I saw the few bare bones on His back. The meek Jesus moaned softly and sighed…. (188) My heart almost stopped at the sight of these tortures. The Lord said to me, I suffer even greater pain than that which you see. And Jesus gave me to know for what sins He subjected himself to the scourging: these are sins of impurity. Oh, how dreadful was Jesus' moral suffering during the scourging. (445)

Convert me, Jesus, from trying to escape pain, and let me endure pain with Your strength.

Jesus Is Crowned with Thorns

… after the scourging, the torturers took the Lord and stripped him of His own garment, which had already adhered to the wounds; as they took it off, His wounds reopened; then they threw a dirty and tattered scarlet cloak over the fresh wounds of the Lord. The cloak, in some places, barely reached His knees. They made Him sit on a piece of beam. And then they wove a crown of thorns, which they put on His sacred head. They put a reed in His hand and made fun of Him, bowing to Him as to a king. Some spat in His face, while others took the reed and struck Him on the head with it.

Others caused him pain by slapping Him; still others covered His face and struck Him with their fists. Jesus bore all this with meekness. Who can comprehend Him — comprehend His suffering? Jesus' eyes were downcast. I sensed what was happening in the most sweet Heart of Jesus at that time. Let every soul reflect on what Jesus was suffering at that moment. They tried to outdo each other in insulting the Lord. I reflected: Where does such malice in man come from?

It is caused by sin. Love and sin have met. (408)

Convert me, Jesus, from acting with false pride, and let me be humble like You.

Jesus Is Condemned to Death

[Jesus said to St. Faustina:] Consider My sufferings before Pilate. (149)

Jesus was suddenly standing before me, stripped of His clothes, His body completely covered with wounds, His eyes flooded with tears and blood, His face disfigured and covered with spittle. (268)

> "When I see Jesus tormented, my heart is torn to pieces, and I think: what will become of sinners if they do not take advantage of the Passion of Jesus: In His Passion, I see a whole sea of mercy." (948)

Convert me, Jesus, from denying my cross. Let me accept whatever You ask of me.

Jesus Carries His Cross

Obedient to His Father's will, the Lord bore His cross on the road to Calvary. We, too, must bear our cross in humble obedience to God.

The moment I knelt down to cross out my own will, as the Lord had bid me to do, I heard this voice in my soul: From today on, do not fear God's judgment, for you will not be judged. (374)

True love of God consists in carrying out God's will. To show God our love in what we do, all our actions, even the least, must spring from our love of God. (279)

Convert me, Jesus, from rejecting my burdens, and let me carry them confidently in You.

Jesus Falls the First Time

Exhausted by beatings and torture, Jesus stumbled to the ground under the weight of the cross.

> After the confession, I meditated on Jesus' terrible Passion, and I understood that what I was suffering was nothing compared to the Savior's Passion, and that even the smallest imperfection was the cause of this terrible suffering. Then my soul was filled with very great contrition, and only then I sensed that I was in the sea of the unfathomable mercy of God. Oh, how few words I have to express what I am experiencing! I feel I am like a drop of dew engulfed in the depths of the bottomless ocean of divine mercy. (654)
>
> I united my sufferings with the sufferings of Jesus and offered them for myself and for the conversion of souls who do not trust in the goodness of God. (323)

Convert me, Jesus, from ignoring my imperfections, and let me be perfected by Your love.

Jesus Meets His Mother

O Mary, today a terrible sword has pierced Your holy soul. Except for God, no one knows of Your suffering. Your soul does not break; it is brave because it is with Jesus. Sweet Mother, unite my soul to Jesus, because it is only then that I will be able to endure all trials and tribulations, and only in union with Jesus, will my little sacrifices be pleasing to God. (915)

Convert me, Jesus, from forgetting your Mother, and let me come closer to You through Mary.

Simon the Cyrene Helps Jesus Carry His Cross

When we humbly accept our crosses, like Simon, we share in a small way the pain Jesus endured for us.

> One sister said to me, "Get ready, Sister, to receive a small cross, at the hands of Mother Superior. I feel sorry for you." But as for me, I rejoiced at this in the depths of my soul and had been ready for it for a long time. When she saw my courage, she was surprised. I see now that a soul cannot do much of itself, but with God it can do all things. Behold what God's grace can do. Few are the souls that are always watchful for divine graces, and even fewer of such souls who follow those inspirations faithfully. (138)

Convert me, Jesus, from being a passive spectator, and let me participate actively in your Passion.

Veronica Wipes the Face of Jesus

When Veronica wiped the bloodied face of the Lord, He lovingly left the imprint of His face on her veil. As I meditate with sorrow on His horrific Passion, with St. Faustina I seek His imprint on my heart.

> I want to resemble You, O Jesus, — You crucified, tortured, and humiliated. Jesus, imprint upon my heart and soul Your own humility. (267)
>
> I am learning how to be good from Jesus, from Him who is goodness itself, so that I might be called a daughter of the heavenly Father. (669)

Convert me, Jesus, from indifference to the poor, and let me see Your face in all those in need.

Jesus Falls the Second Time

When Jesus falls again, His executioners give Him no help. Rather they strike Him with rods and whips.

> Jesus, do not leave me alone in suffering. You know, Lord, how weak I am. I am an abyss of wretchedness, I am nothingness itself; so what will be so strange if You leave me alone and I fall? I am an infant, Lord, so I cannot get along by myself. However, beyond all abandonment I trust…. (1489)

Convert me, Jesus, from the many occasions of sin, and let me flee from all temptation.

Jesus Consoles the Women of Jerusalem

Just as Jesus encouraged the women on the way to Calvary, so He encourages us when we meditate sorrowfully on His Passion and when we feel discouragement.

> I fervently beg the Lord to strengthen my faith, so that in my drab, everyday life I will not be guided by human dispositions, but by those of the spirit…. [L]ively faith maintains the soul in the higher regions and assigns self-love its proper place, that is to say, the lowest one. (210)

> O sinner, you must not doubt or despair,
> But trust in mercy, for you also can become holy. (522)

Convert me, Jesus, from sorrow and despair, and let me trust that You safeguard me from evil.

Jesus Falls the Third Time

When Jesus fell a third time, the crowd jeered, but He entrusted himself to His Father's everlasting arms, got up, and doggedly made His way to Golgotha. We do well to imitate His trust when we fall in our daily battle.

My Jesus, despite Your graces, I see and feel all my misery. I begin my day with battle and end it with battle. As soon as I conquer one obstacle, ten more appear to take its place. But I am not worried, because I know that this is the time of struggle, not peace. When the burden of the battle becomes too much for me, I throw myself like a child into the arms of the heavenly Father and trust I will not perish. O my Jesus, how prone I am to evil, and this forces me to be constantly vigilant. But I do not lose heart. I trust God's grace, which abounds in the worst misery. (606)

Convert me, Jesus, from serious sins, and let me confess my guilt and receive your pardon.

Jesus Is Stripped of His Garments and Nailed to the Cross

Between this radiance and the earth I saw Jesus, nailed to the Cross in such a way that when God wanted to look at the earth, He had to look through the wounds of Jesus. And I understood that it was for the sake of Jesus that God blesses the earth. (60)

Then I saw Jesus Crucified and He said to me, It is in My Passion that you must seek light and strength. (654)

O my Jesus, my only hope, thank You for the book which you have opened before my soul's eyes. That book is Your Passion which You underwent for love of me. It is from this book that I have learned how to love God and souls. In this book there are found for us inexhaustible treasures. O Jesus, how few souls understand You in Your martyrdom of love! Oh, how great is the fire of purest love which burns in Your Most Sacred Heart! Happy the soul that has come to understand the love of the Heart of Jesus! (304)

Convert me, Jesus, from anxiety about divine judgment, and let me make amends for my sins.

Jesus' Thirst for Souls

Good Friday. At three o'clock, I saw the Lord Jesus, crucified, who looked at me and said, I thirst. Then I saw two rays issue from His side, just as they appear in the image. I then felt in my soul the desire to save souls and to empty myself for the sake of poor sinners. I offered myself, together with the dying Jesus, to the Eternal Father, for the salvation of the whole world. With Jesus, through Jesus and in Jesus is my communion with You, Eternal Father. (648)

Convert me, Jesus, from satisfying my own desires, and let me thirst for justice for all.

Jesus Dies on the Cross

[Jesus said to St. Faustina:] When I was dying on the cross, I was not thinking about Myself, but about poor sinners, and I prayed for them to My Father. I want your last moments to be completely similar to

Mine on the cross. There is but one price at which souls are bought, and that is suffering united to My suffering on the cross. Pure love understands these words; carnal love will never understand them. (324)

O merciful Jesus, stretched on the cross, be mindful of the hour of our death. O most merciful Heart of Jesus, opened with a lance, shelter me at the last moment of my life. O Blood and Water, which gushed forth from the Heart of Jesus as a fount of unfathomable mercy for me at the hour of my death, O dying Jesus, Hostage of mercy, avert the Divine wrath at the hour of my death. (813)

"When I make the Way of the Cross, I am deeply moved at the twelfth station. Here I reflect on the omnipotence of God's mercy which passed through the Heart of Jesus." (1309)

Convert me, Jesus, from clinging to my life, and let me give my soul to You.

Jesus Is Pierced with a Lance

Today I saw the Crucified Lord Jesus. Precious pearls and diamonds were pouring forth from the wound in His Heart. I saw how a multitude of souls was gathering these gifts, but there was one soul who was closest to His Heart and she, knowing the greatness of these gifts, was gathering them with liberality, not only for herself, but for others as well. The Savior said to me, Behold, the treasures of grace that flow down upon souls, but not all souls know how to take advantage of My generosity. (1687)

In this open wound of the Heart of Jesus I enclose all poor humans ... and those individuals whom I love, as often as I make the Way of the Cross. From that Fount of Mercy issued the two rays, that is, the Blood and the Water. With the immensity of their grace they flood the whole world.... (1309)

Convert me, Jesus, from greed and selfishness, and let me become meek and humble of heart.

Jesus Is Taken Down from the Cross and Laid in the Tomb

The world still has no idea of all that Jesus suffered. (1054) You expired, Jesus, but the source of life gushed forth for souls, and the ocean of mercy opened up for the whole world. O Fount of Life, unfathomable Divine Mercy, envelop the whole world and empty Yourself out upon us. (1319)

Convert me, Jesus, from fear of dying, and let me embrace death as my full pathway to You.

Jesus Rises from the Dead

Easter [April 17, 1938]. During Mass, I thanked the Lord Jesus for having deigned to redeem us and for having given us that greatest of all gifts; namely, His love in Holy Communion; that is, His very own Self. At that moment, I was drawn into the bosom of the Most Holy Trinity, and I was immersed in the love of the Father, the Son and the Holy Spirit. These moments are hard to describe. (1670)

Triduum Prayers

O Jesus, Stretched Out upon the Cross

O Jesus, stretched out upon the cross, I implore You, give me the grace of doing faithfully the most holy will of Your Father, in all things, always and everywhere. And when this will of God will seem to me very harsh and difficult to fulfill, it is then I beg You, Jesus, may power and strength flow upon me from Your wounds, and may my lips keep repeating, "Your will be done, O Lord." O Savior of the world, Lover of man's salvation, who in such terrible torment and pain forget Yourself to think only of the salvation of souls, O most compassionate Jesus, grant me the grace to forget myself that I may live totally for souls, helping You in the work of salvation, according to the most holy will of Your Father.... (1265)

St. Clare of Assisi's Litany of the Sacred Wounds

Jesus told St. Faustina the immense value of meditating on His sacred wounds. He said to her that "... the contemplation of My painful wounds is of great profit to you, and it brings Me great joy" (369).

To fix our gaze and meditate on Jesus' sacred wounds is of infinite value for all sinners. Never let the Passion of Jesus be far from your prayers.

This devotion is a powerful meditation that helps us better recognize our own faults and failings while, at the same time, offering the hope of being delivered from sin and evil — past, present, and future.

Like St. Faustina, we can flee to His wounds of mercy and healing.

St. Clare's litany ends with the wound in Christ's side. Pious tradition holds that after Longinus pierced him with a spear, immediately the Roman soldier was healed of his partial blindness when some of the blood and water from Jesus' side fell into his eyes. St. Longinus converted and became a monk in Cappadocia, where he later was martyred for the Faith.

As I was praying before the Blessed Sacrament and greeting the five wounds of Jesus, at each salutation I felt a torrent of graces gushing into my soul, giving me a foretaste of heaven and absolute confidence in God's mercy. (1337)

———

"During Mass, I suffered pain in my body: in my hands, my feet and my side. Jesus is sending me this kind of suffering that I may make reparation for sinners. (942) His Passion was imprinted on my body in an invisible manner, but no less painfully. (964) In difficult moments I must take refuge in the wounds of Jesus; I must seek consolation, comfort, light, and affirmation in the wounds of Jesus." (226)

To the Wound in the Right Hand

Praise and honor be given You, O my Lord Jesus Christ, by reason of the Sacred Wound in Your Right Hand. **By this adorable wound, I beseech You to pardon me all the sins I have committed by thoughts, words, and deeds, by neglect in Your service, and by self-indulgence, both waking and sleeping.** *Grant me the grace that, by a devout and frequent remembrance of Your Holy Passion, I may honor Your sacred wounds and the death which You endured for love of me, and that, by chastising my body, I may testify my gratitude for Your sufferings and Your death. Who lives and reigns, world without end. Amen.*

Our Father, Hail Mary.

To the Wound in the Left Hand

Praise and honor be given you, O most amiable Jesus, by reason of the Sacred Wound in Your Left Hand. **By this holy wound, I beseech You to have pity on me to change within me whatever is displeasing to You.** *Grant me to be victorious over my enemies, so that, by the power of Your grace, I may overcome them; and do You, by Your holy and adorable death, deliver me from all dangers, present and to come, and make me worthy to share the glory of Your Blessed Kingdom. Who lives and reigns, world without end. Amen.*

Our Father, Hail Mary.

To the Wound of the Right Foot

Praise and honor be given You, O sweetest Jesus, by reason of the Sacred Wound in Your Right Foot. **By this holy and adorable wound, I beseech You, to enable me to bring forth worthy fruits of penance for my sins.** *I humbly entreat You, for the sake of Your adorable death, to keep me, day and night, in Your holy will, to preserve me from all adversity of soul and body, and, on the dreadful day of judgment, to deal with me according to Your mercy, that I may obtain eternal joys. Who lives and reigns, world without end. Amen.*

Our Father, Hail Mary.

To the Wound of the Left Foot

Praise and honor be given You, O sweet Jesus, by reason of the Sacred Wound on Your Left Foot. **By this adorable wound, I beseech You to grant me pardon and full remission of all my sins, so that, with Your aid, I may escape the rigors of justice.** *I entreat You, O good and merciful Jesus, for the sake of Your holy death, to grant that at the hour of my death, I may have the grace to confess my sins with a perfect contrition, to receive the adorable Sacrament of Your Body* and Your Blood, and likewise, the Holy Sacrament of the Sick for my eternal salvation. Who lives and reigns, world without end. Amen.

Our Father, Hail Mary.

To the Wound in the Sacred Side

Praise and honor be given You, O good and sweetest Jesus, by reason of the Wound in Your Sacred Side. **By this adorable wound and by that immense mercy shown Longinus and to us all, in allowing Your Sacred Side to be opened, I beseech You, O good Jesus, that as in Baptism You purified me from original sin, so now You would be pleased, by the merits of Your Most Precious Blood, which is offered up this day over the whole world, to deliver me from all evils, past, present, and to come.** I entreat You, by Your bitter death, to give me a lively faith, a firm hope, and perfect charity, so that I may love You with my whole heart, with my whole soul, and with all my strength. Uphold me by Your grace in the practice of good works, so that I may persevere to the end in Your holy service and glorify You in time and eternity. Amen.

Our Father, Hail Mary.

We adore You, O Christ, and we bless You, because by Your death and Your precious Blood, You have redeemed the world.

O Almighty Eternal God, who has ransomed the human race by the five wounds of Your Son, Our Lord and Savior Jesus Christ, we beseech You, by the merits of His precious Blood, to grant unto us, who, each day, venerate these same adorable wounds, to be delivered from a sudden and unprovided death. Through the same Jesus Christ, Your Son, our Lord, who lives and reigns with You, in the unity of the Holy Spirit, one God, now and for ever. Amen.

Into Your Hands

O God, all hearts are in Your Hands. You can bend, as it pleases You, the most stubborn, and soften the most obstinate. I beseech You by the Holy Name, the precious Blood, the Merits, Wounds, and Divine Heart of Jesus, Your Beloved Son, to grant the conversion we ask. Amen.

The Seven Offerings of the Precious Blood

The Blood of Jesus, like His wounds, deserves special honor because of its relationship to the sacred Passion. This devotion began with the apostles, who speak of the precious Blood, the price of our redemption. Offer the Blood of Jesus in expiation for sin, for the conversion of sinners, for the needs of our Church, and for the souls in purgatory.

———

Immaculate Heart of Mary, offer to the Eternal Father the precious Blood of Our Lord Jesus Christ, for the conversion of sinners, especially (name).

Eternal Father, *we offer You the precious Blood of Jesus, poured out on the cross and offered daily on the altar, for the glory of Your name, for the coming of Your kingdom, for the salvation of all people.*

> *Glory be to the Father, and to the Son, and to the Holy Spirit,*
> *as it was in the beginning, is now, and ever shall be, world without end.*
> *Amen.*
> *Praise and thanksgiving be evermore to Jesus,*
> *who with His blood has saved us.*

Eternal Father, *we offer You the precious Blood of Jesus, poured out on the cross and offered daily on the altar, for the spread of the Church, for Pope N.,* *for bishops, priests, and religious, and for the sanctification of all the people of God.*

Glory be ... Praise and thanksgiving ...

Eternal Father, *we offer You the precious Blood of Jesus, poured out on the cross and offered daily on the altar, for the conversion of sinners, for the loving acceptance of Your Word, and for the union of all Christians.*

Glory be ... Praise and thanksgiving ...

Eternal Father, *we offer You the precious Blood of Jesus, poured out on the cross and offered daily on the altar, for our civil authorities, for the strengthening of public morals, and for peace and justice among all nations.*

Glory be ... Praise and thanksgiving ...

Eternal Father, *we offer You the precious Blood of Jesus, poured out on the cross and offered daily on the altar, for the sanctification of our work and our suffering, for the poor, the sick and the afflicted, and for all who rely on our prayers.*

Glory be ... Praise and thanksgiving ...

Eternal Father, *we offer You the precious Blood of Jesus, poured out on the cross and offered daily on the altar, for our own special needs, both spiritual and temporal, for those of our relatives, friends, and benefactors, and also for those of our enemies.*

Glory be ... Praise and thanksgiving ...

Eternal Father, *we offer You the precious Blood of Jesus, poured out on the cross and offered daily on the altar, for those who are to die this day, for the souls in purgatory, and for our final union with Christ in glory.*

Glory be ... Praise and thanksgiving ...

The Golden Arrow Devotion

Devotion to the Holy Face originated on the way to Calvary, when Our Lord himself imprinted the outline of His blood-stained countenance on Veronica's veil.

The purpose of the Holy Face devotion is to show honor and reverence to the adorable face of Jesus, disfigured in His Passion, to make reparation and to obtain the conversion of those who profane the Lord's Day. Gazing upon the face of Christ crucified unites us with all His sorrows, love, and total abandonment.

Our Lord, in visions to Sister Marie of St. Peter, a Carmelite, requested that a devotion to His Holy Face be established. He gave her the "Golden Arrow" prayer as a remedy to the "poisoned arrows" of blasphemy. She saw the Sacred Heart of Jesus, in a vision, as torrents of grace streamed from it for the conversion of sinners. He said to her: "Every time My Face is contemplated I will pour out My Love into the hearts of those persons, and by means of My Holy Face the salvation of many souls will be obtained."

My Jesus, to atone for blasphemers I will keep silent when unjustly reprimanded and in this way make partial amends to You. (81)

The Golden Arrow Prayer

May the most holy, most sacred, most adorable, most incomprehensible and ineffable Name of God be forever praised, blessed, loved, adored and glorified in Heaven, on earth, and under the earth, by all the creatures of God, and by the Sacred Heart of Our Lord Jesus Christ, in the Most Holy Sacrament of the Altar. Amen.

Eternal Father, I offer Thee the adorable Face of Thy beloved Son Jesus for the honor and glory of Thy Name, for the conversion of sinners and the salvation of the dying. Amen.

Oh, Jesus, through the merits of your Holy Face, have pity on us, and on the whole world. (Three times)

St. Thérèse of Lisieux's Prayer to the Divine Face

St. Faustina had a great devotion to St. Thérèse, who appeared to her in a dream. St. Thérèse composed this prayer as an Act of Reparation to the Holy Face for the conversion of sinners. St. Faustina's desire to make Jesus loved and save souls is also echoed in this beautiful prayer.

—

O Jesus, who in your cruel Passion became the "Reproach of men and the Man of Sorrows," I worship Your Divine Face. Once it shined with the beauty and sweetness of the Divinity. Now for my sake it has become as the face of a "leper." Yet in that disfigured face, I recognize Your infinite love, and I am consumed with the desire of loving You and of making You loved by all mankind. The tears that streamed in such abundance from Your eyes are to me as precious pearls which I delight to gather, that with their infinite worth I may ransom the souls of poor sinners. Amen.

Prayer to Jesus Crucified

When pain overwhelms my soul,
And the horizon darkens like night,
And the heart is torn with the torment of suffering,
Jesus Crucified, You are my strength.

When the soul, dimmed with pain,
Exerts itself in battle without respite,
And the heart is in agony and torment,
Jesus Crucified, You are the hope of my salvation.

And so the days pass,
As the soul bathes in a sea of bitterness,
And the heart dissolves in tears,
Jesus Crucified, You shine for me like the dawn.

And when the cup of bitterness brims over,
And all things conspire against her,
And the soul goes down to the Garden of Olives,
Jesus Crucified, in You is my defense.

When the soul, conscious of its innocence,
Accepts these dispensations from God,
The heart can then repay hurts with love.
Jesus Crucified, transform my weakness into omnipotence. (1151)

XI. Acts of the Apostles, Acts of Conversion

"Go into all the world and preach the gospel to the whole creation."
— Mark 16:15

The apostles, filled with the Holy Spirit, began immediately to preach the Gospel. Many people that they encountered put faith in Jesus and changed their lives. They turned away from sin and turned to God. The Acts of the Apostles records the conversion experiences of these earliest Christians. Reflect on their conversions, take them as models for your trans-

COMMISSIONED FOR CONVERSIONS

"May 26, [1938 — Feast of the Ascension]. Today I accompanied the Lord Jesus as He ascended into heaven. It was about noon. I was overcome by a great longing for God. It is a strange thing, the more I felt God's presence, the more ardently I desired Him. Then I saw myself in the midst of a huge crowd of disciples and apostles, together with the Mother of God. Jesus was telling them to ... Go out into the whole world and teach in My name. He stretched out His hands and blessed them and disappeared in a cloud. I saw the longing of Our Lady. Her soul yearned for Jesus, with the whole force of Her love. But She was so peaceful and so united to the will of God that there was not a stir in Her heart but for what God wanted." (1710)

Convert me, Jesus, from doubting Your presence; let me evangelize all in Your name.

formation, and pray for the faith to respond to Christ's invitation to change and for the grace to do it.

ACTS 1: Luke lists the names of the eleven apostles, all of whom were converts called by Jesus: "Peter and John and James and Andrew, Philip and Thomas, Bartholomew and Matthew, James the son of Alphaeus and Simon the Zealot and Judas the son of James" (v. 13). Then, by lot, Matthias is chosen for "this ministry and apostleship from which Judas turned aside" (v. 25), while "Joseph called Barsabbas, who was surnamed Justus" (v. 23), continues as a disciple (and later a saint).

Lord, help me to deny myself, take up my cross, and follow You as Your disciple. Holy Apostles, intercede for us!

ACTS 4: "Joseph who was surnamed by the apostles Barnabas (which means, Son of encouragement), a Levite, a native of Cyprus, sold a field which belonged to him" and brought the money and laid it "at the apostles' feet" (vv. 36-37). He later sought out Paul in Damascus and introduced him to the apostles in Jerusalem.

Lord, teach me how to reach out to others and to be generous with what I have. St. Barnabas, intercede for us!

ACTS 5: Gamaliel — a teacher of the law, who probably taught the Law to the Pharisee Saul (known later as Paul) — tells the Sanhedrin that "if this plan or this undertaking is of men, it will fail; but if it is of God, you will not be able to overthrow them. You might even be found opposing God!" (vv. 38-39). Gamaliel will eventually be baptized and become a saint.

Lord, show me how to discern right from wrong and to obey all Your commands. St. Gamaliel, intercede for us!

ACTS 6: Nicolaus of Antioch, a convert from Judaism, is presented along with six others (Stephen, Philip, Prochorus, Nicanor, Timon, and Parmenas), acknowledged to be "men of good repute, full of the Spirit and of wisdom" (v. 5), and they become servants (later formally called deacons) to aid the poor.

Lord, make me a prudent servant of those who are most vulnerable and in need of Your care. Saintly converts, intercede for us!

ACTS 8: Philip, the deacon, travels to Samaria and encounters an Ethiopian eunuch (a treasurer to Queen Candace) and asks: "Do you understand what you are reading?" (v. 30). Philip explains to him the Scriptures and baptizes him at once.

Lord, enable me to witness to Your Sacred Word and lead people to new life. St. Philip, intercede for us!

ACTS 8: Simon the Magician, at first trying to impress others with his false powers, comes to believe in "the kingdom of God and the name of Jesus Christ" (v. 12), is baptized like the rest, and becomes a devoted follower of Philip.

Lord, curb me from vanity and direct my powers to bringing good into this world. Saintly Simon, intercede for us!

ACTS 9: Saul, pursuing Christian believers, is knocked down and hears a voice saying: "I am Jesus, whom you are persecuting; but rise and enter the city and you will be told what you are to do" (vv. 5-6).

Lord, let me respond to Your call to build up — rather than tear down — my Christian faith. St. Paul, intercede for us!

ACTS 9: Ananias, to whom the Lord had appeared in a vision, fears meeting Saul but finally complies with Jesus' direction: "Go, for he is a chosen instrument of mine to carry my name before the Gentiles and kings and the sons of Israel" (v. 15). Ananias cures Paul of his blindness and baptizes him in the Holy Spirit.

Lord, eradicate my fears and anoint me with the oil of gladness among my fellow Christians. St. Ananias, intercede for us!

ACTS 9: Peter finds "a man named Aeneas, who had been bedridden for eight years and was paralyzed" and immediately cures him in Jesus' name, telling him: "Rise and make your bed" (vv. 33-34). Then, "all the residents of Lydda and Sharon saw him, and they turned to the Lord" (v. 35).

Lord, cast out from me any physical or mental paralysis and restore my personal well-being. Saintly Aeneas, intercede for us!

ACTS 9: Some disciples near Joppa urgently request Peter to "come to us without delay" (v. 38) to view the body of "a disciple named Tabitha, which means Dorcas or Gazelle" (v. 36). Peter raises her from the dead, and this miracle causes many to come to believe in the Lord.

Lord, do not delay in fulfilling my hopes and in providing me with life everlasting. St. Tabitha, intercede for us!

ACTS 10: "Cornelius, a centurion" living in Caesarea, was "a devout man who feared God with all his household, [and] gave alms liberally to the people, and prayed constantly to God" (vv. 1-2). Peter's vision of accepting the Gentiles' faith leads the apostle to "preach forgiveness of sins through

[Jesus'] name"; suddenly, "the Holy Spirit fell on all who heard the word" (vv. 43-44), and Cornelius and those with him are baptized.

Lord, direct me to be inclusive of all people who seek the Way, the Truth, and the Life. Saintly Cornelius, intercede for us!

ACTS 13: "Now in the church at Antioch there were prophets and teachers, Barnabas, Simeon who was called Niger, Lucius of Cyrene, Manaen a member of the court of Herod the tetrarch, and Saul" (v. 1). While they prayed and fasted, "the Holy Spirit said, 'Set apart for me Barnabas and Saul for the work to which I have called them' " (v. 2). The community "laid their hands on them and sent them off" (v. 3).

Lord, by the grace of the Holy Spirit, send me forth to do Your work wherever You wish. Saintly converts, intercede for us!

ACTS 16: Paul arrives in Lystra to meet "a disciple … named Timothy" (v. 1) — whose mother, Eunice, and grandmother, Lois, converted him to the faith. He joins Paul and "they delivered to them for observance the decisions which had been reached by the apostles and elders who were at Jerusalem. So the churches were strengthened in the faith, and they increased in numbers daily" (vv. 4-5).

Lord, give me family and friends to support me in living according to the Church's teachings. St. Timothy, intercede for us!

ACTS 16: Paul preaches outside of Philippi, and one who listened was "a woman named Lydia, … a seller of purple goods" (v. 14). When she and her household have been baptized, she invites Paul (who was convinced of her beliefs) to stay at her house.

Lord, embolden my convictions so I can invite others to learn about my faith in You. St. Lydia, intercede for us!

ACTS 16: When Paul and Silas are freed from their prison, the jailer asks: "What must I do to be saved?" (v. 30). Learning about Jesus, the jailer and his family are baptized, after which he "set food before them; and he rejoiced with all his household that he had believed in God" (v. 34).

Lord, bring all my family, members whether by blood or by marriage, into the Church. Sts. Paul and Silas, intercede for us!

ACTS 17: Hearing Paul's talk about the "unknown god" (v. 23), Dionysius (a member of the court of the Areopagus), a woman named Damaris, and several others listen to Paul's instruction. In Thessalonica, Paul stays at the house of Jason whom a crowd "dragged ... [with] some of the brethren before the city authorities, crying, 'These men who have turned the world upside down have come here also, and Jason has received them; and they are all acting against the decrees of Caesar, saying that there is another king, Jesus' " (vv. 6-7).

Lord, instruct me in the reality of the kingdom of our God as Father, Son, and Holy Spirit. Saintly Damaris, pray for us!

ACTS 18: In Corinth, "a Jew named Aquila" and "his wife Priscilla" (v. 1) collaborate with Paul in tent making. There Paul decides that he "will go to the Gentiles" and lodges at "the house of a man named Titius Justus, a worshiper of God" (vv. 6-7). Next door, "Crispus, the ruler of the synagogue, believed in the Lord, together with all his household; and many of the Corinthians hearing Paul believed and were baptized" (v. 8).

Lord, connect me in good relationships with people who exemplify fidelity to Your love. Saintly Aquila and Priscilla, intercede for us!

ACTS 19: A ship brought to Ephesus "a Jew named Apollos," who was "well versed in the scriptures [and] had been instructed in the way of the Lord" (vv. 24-25) — which Priscilla and Aquila then explained in more detail. Apollos "greatly helped those who through grace had believed ... [and showed] by the scriptures that the Christ was Jesus" (v. 27-28).

Lord, expand my understanding of the Scriptures that reveal Your powerful presence. Saintly Apollos, intercede for us!

ACTS 19: In Ephesus, "some itinerant Jewish exorcists" invoke "the name of the Lord Jesus over those who had evil spirits" (v. 13); however, they fail miserably and are beaten by a demoniac. Still, "fear fell upon them all; and the name of the Lord Jesus was extolled" (v. 17).

Lord, I acknowledge You as stronger than any sort of evil and the conqueror of the devil.

ACTS 20: Paul was accompanied by many disciples to Troas: "Sopater of Beroea, the son of Pyrrhus ...; and of the Thessalonians, Aristarchus and Secundus; and Gaius of Derbe, and Timothy; and the Asians, Tychicus and Trophimus" (v. 4). There "a young man named Eutychus was sitting in the window," listening to Paul (v. 9); becoming drowsy, he fell three stories to the ground and died. Paul clutched the boy to himself, saying: "Do not be alarmed, for his life is in him" (v. 10). So, "they took the lad away alive, and were not a little comforted" (v. 12).

Lord, let me accompany You in the people we meet, however dangerous or difficult it may be. Saintly Eutychus, intercede for us!

ACTS 27: At Caesarea, "Paul and some other prisoners" were handed over to a centurion named Julius, who, at the port of Sidon, "kindly … gave [Paul] leave to go to his friends and be cared for" (vv. 1, 3). Severe storms almost sank the ship (with its 276 passengers aboard); nevertheless, Paul warned the centurion to keep his men on the ship lest they perish. For food, "he took bread, and giving thanks to God in the presence of all he broke it and began to eat," and "they all were encouraged and ate some food themselves" (vv. 35-36).

Lord, feed me with your Body and Blood, which encourages me to fear nothing when I am by Your side. Saintly Julius, intercede for us!

ACTS 28: On Malta "were lands belonging to the chief man of the island, named Publius" (v. 7), who provided Paul food and lodging for three days. In return, Paul cured Publius' father of chronic fever and dysentery, and he cured many other sick people on the island who were brought to him.

Lord, heal me of earthly afflictions and turn my gratitude into joy we can share with others. Saintly Publius, intercede for us!

XII. A Novena to the Divine Mercy for the Conversion of the World

On Good Friday, 1937, Jesus requested that St. Faustina make a special novena. "… I am to begin it for the conversion of the whole world and for the recognition of The Divine Mercy … *[Jesus then tells St. Faustina]* … so that every soul will praise My goodness. I desire trust from My creatures. Encourage souls to place great trust in My fathomless mercy. Let the weak, sinful soul have no fear to approach Me, for even if it had more sins than there are grains of sand in the world, all would be drowned in the unmeasurable depths of My mercy" (1059).

The Lord dictated the intentions for each day. Faustina was to bring to His heart a different group of souls each day and immerse them in the ocean of His mercy.

First Day

[Jesus:] Today, bring to Me all mankind, especially all sinners.... (1210)

———

Most Merciful Jesus, whose very nature it is to have compassion on us and to forgive us, do not look upon our sins but upon our trust which we place in Your infinite goodness. Receive us all into the abode of Your Most Compassion-

[Jesus said to St. Faustina:] "I desire that during these nine days you bring souls to the fountain of My mercy, that they may draw therefrom strength and refreshment and whatever grace they need in the hardships of life, and especially at the hour of death." (1209)

ate Heart, and never let us escape from it. We beg this of You by Your love which unites You to the Father and the Holy Spirit....

Eternal Father, turn Your merciful gaze upon all mankind and especially upon poor sinners, all enfolded in the Most Compassionate Heart of Jesus. For the sake of His sorrowful Passion, show us Your mercy, that we may praise the omnipotence of Your mercy forever and ever. Amen. (1211)

Second Day

[Jesus:] Today bring to Me the souls of priests and religious.... (1212)

———

Most merciful Jesus, from whom comes all that is good, increase Your grace in us, that we may perform worthy works of mercy, and that all who see them may glorify the Father of Mercy who is in heaven....

Eternal Father, turn Your merciful gaze upon the company [of chosen ones] in Your vineyard — upon the souls of priests and religious; and endow them with the strength of Your blessing. For the love of the Heart of Your Son in which they are enfolded, impart to them Your power and light, that they may be able to guide others in the way of salvation, and with one voice sing praise to Your boundless mercy for ages without end. Amen. (1213)

Third Day

[Jesus:] Today bring to Me all devout and faithful souls.... (1214)

———

Most Merciful Jesus, from the treasury of Your mercy You impart Your graces in great abundance to each and all. Receive us into the abode of Your Most Compassionate Heart and never let us escape from it. We beg this of You by that most wondrous love for the heavenly Father with which Your Heart burns so fiercely....

Eternal Father, turn Your merciful gaze upon faithful souls, as upon the inheritance of Your Son. For the sake of His sorrowful Passion, grant them Your blessing and surround them with Your constant protection. Thus may they never fail in love or lose the treasure of the holy faith, but rather, with all the hosts of Angels and Saints, may they glorify Your boundless mercy for endless ages. Amen. (1215)

Fourth Day

[Jesus:] Today bring to Me the pagans and those who do not yet know Me.... (1216)

———

Most Compassionate Jesus, You are the Light of the whole world. Receive into the abode of Your Most Compassionate Heart the souls of pagans who as yet do not know You. Let the rays of Your grace enlighten them that they, too, together with us, may extol Your wonderful mercy; and do not let them escape from the abode which is Your Most Compassionate Heart....

Eternal Father, turn Your merciful gaze upon the souls of pagans and of those who as yet do not know You, but who are enclosed in the Most Compassionate Heart of Jesus. Draw them to the light of the Gospel. These souls do not know what great happiness it is to love You. Grant that they, too, may extol the generosity of Your mercy for endless ages. Amen. (1217)

Fifth Day

[Jesus:] Today bring to Me the souls of the heretics and schismatics.... (1218)

———

Most Merciful Jesus, Goodness Itself, You do not refuse light to those who seek it of You. Receive into the abode of Your Most Compassionate Heart the souls of heretics and schismatics. Draw them by Your light into the unity of the Church, and do not let them escape from the abode of Your Most Compassionate Heart; but bring it about that they, too, come to extol the generosity of Your mercy....

Eternal Father, turn Your merciful gaze upon the souls of heretics and schismatics, who have squandered Your blessings and misused Your graces by obstinately persisting in their errors. Do not look upon their errors, but upon the love of Your own Son and upon His bitter Passion, which He underwent for their sake, since they, too, are enclosed in the Most Compassionate Heart of Jesus. Bring it about that they also may glorify Your great mercy for endless ages. Amen. (1219)

Sixth Day

[Jesus:] Today bring to Me the meek and humble souls and the souls of little children.... (1220)

———

Most Merciful Jesus, You Yourself have said, "Learn from Me for I am meek and humble of heart." Receive into the abode of Your Most Compassionate Heart all meek and humble souls and the souls of little children. These souls send all heaven into ecstasy and they are the heavenly Father's favorites. They are a sweet-smelling bouquet before the throne of God; God Himself takes delight in their fragrance. These souls have a permanent abode in Your Most Compassionate Heart, O Jesus, and they unceasingly sing out a hymn of love and mercy.... (1221)

Eternal Father, turn Your merciful gaze upon meek souls and humble souls, and upon the souls of little children who are enfolded in the abode which is the Most Compassionate Heart of Jesus. These souls bear the closest resemblance to Your Son. Their fragrance rises from the earth and reaches Your very throne. Father of mercy and of all goodness, I beg You by the love You bear these souls and by the delight You take in them: Bless the whole world, that all souls together may sing out the praises of Your mercy for endless ages. Amen. (1223)

Seventh Day

[Jesus:] Today bring to Me the souls who especially venerate and glorify My mercy.... (1224)

———

Most Merciful Jesus, whose Heart is Love Itself, receive into the abode of Your Most Compassionate Heart the souls of those who particularly extol and venerate the greatness of Your mercy. These souls are mighty with the very power of God Himself. In the midst of all afflictions and adversities they go forward, confident of Your mercy. These souls are united to Jesus and carry all mankind on their shoulders. These souls will not be judged severely, but Your mercy will embrace them as they depart from this life....

Eternal Father, turn Your merciful gaze upon the souls who glorify and venerate Your greatest attribute, that of Your fathomless mercy, and who are enclosed in the Most Compassionate Heart of Jesus. These souls are a living Gospel; their hands are full of deeds of mercy, and their spirit, overflowing with joy, sings a canticle of mercy to You, O Most High! I beg You, O God: Show them Your mercy according to the hope and trust they have placed in You. Let there be accomplished in them the promise of Jesus, who said to them, I Myself will defend as My own glory, during their lifetime, and especially at the hour of their death, those souls who will venerate My fathomless mercy. (1225)

Eighth Day

[Jesus:] Today bring to Me the souls who are in the prison of Purgatory.... (1226)

———

Most Merciful Jesus, You Yourself have said that You desire mercy; so I bring into the abode of Your Most Compassionate Heart the souls in Purgatory, souls who are very dear to You, and yet, who must make retribution to Your justice. May the streams of Blood and Water which gushed forth from Your Heart put out the flames of purifying fire, that in that place, too, the power of Your mercy may be praised....

Eternal Father, turn Your merciful gaze upon the souls suffering in Purgatory, who are enfolded in the Most Compassionate Heart of Jesus. I beg You, by the sorrowful Passion of Jesus Your Son, and by all the bitterness with which His most sacred Soul was flooded, manifest Your mercy to the souls who are under Your just scrutiny. Look upon them in no other way than through the Wounds of Jesus, Your dearly beloved Son; for we firmly believe that there is no limit to Your goodness and compassion. (1227)

Ninth Day

[Jesus:] Today bring to Me souls who have become lukewarm.... (1228)

—

Most compassionate Jesus, You are Compassion Itself. I bring lukewarm souls into the abode of Your Most Compassionate Heart. In this fire of Your pure love let these tepid souls, who, like corpses, filled You with such deep loathing, be once again set aflame. O Most Compassionate Jesus, exercise the omnipotence of Your mercy and draw them into the very ardor of Your love; and bestow upon them the gift of holy love, for nothing is beyond Your power....

Eternal Father, turn Your merciful gaze upon lukewarm souls, who are nonetheless enfolded in the Most Compassionate Heart of Jesus. Father of Mercy, I beg You by the bitter Passion of Your Son and by His three-hour agony on the Cross: Let them, too, glorify the abyss of Your mercy.... (1229)

XIII. INVOKING THE ANGELS FOR CONVERSION

"Behold, I send an angel before you, to guard you on the way and to bring you to the place which I have prepared."
— EXODUS 23-20

St. Faustina's order, the Congregation of Our Lady of Mercy, had a special devotion to the guardian angels, designating them as one of its patrons. Daily prayers and meditations were offered to the angels to protect the sisters against the enemy.

CONFORMED TO THE ANGELS

St. Faustina wanted nothing more than to do the will of God and not offend Him. She was conformed to the holy angels, who, in all they do, reflect only God's greatness, holiness, and will. "I thanked God for His goodness," said Faustina, "that He gives us angels for companions. Oh, how little people reflect on the fact that they always have beside them such a guest, and at the same time a witness to everything! Remember, sinners, that you likewise have a witness to all your deeds" (630).

Our guardian angels' great mission is to see us home in heaven. They pray for us with great love before the throne of God. It has been said that they pass our place in heaven every day. They are intent on obtaining every grace and favor for our eternal welfare.

We must ask their help every day to purify us here on earth so as to avoid purgatory. If we invoke our guardian angels, they will strengthen us against temptation. And they will be a most powerful help at the hour of our death.

Let us be comforted that we are not fighting alone, but that we have the support of God's angelic armies. He has given us these powerful defenders to aid us. Call on them. But let us also remember, with God's help, to continue the fight. No one is crowned without conquering. "Be faithful unto death, and I will give you the crown of life" (Rev 2:10).

Prayer to My Guardian Angel

Angel of God, my guardian dear,
To whom God's love commits me here,
Ever this day, be at my side,
To light and guard, to rule and guide.

Take me by the hand so that I may obey
your guidance, and attain eternal happiness.
Amen.

Supplication to the Angels

Almighty Eternal Triune God, before we implore Your servants, the holy angels, and call upon them for help, we fall on our knees and adore You, Father, Son, and Holy Spirit. Be honored and praised for all eternity, and may all angels and men, whom You created, adore, love, and serve You, O Holy, Mighty, and Immortal God!

You also, Mary, Queen of Angels, graciously accept the supplications we address to your servants. We beg you to bring these our petitions to the throne of the Most High that we may find grace, salvation, and help! Amen.

You great, holy angels, you have been given to us by God for our protection and help! We implore you in the name of the Triune God, hasten to help us!

> *We implore you in the name of the precious Blood of Our Lord Jesus Christ, hasten to help us!*
> *We implore you in the all-powerful name of Jesus, hasten to help us!*
> *We implore you by all the wounds of Our Lord Jesus Christ, hasten to help us!*
> *We implore you by all the sufferings of Our Lord Jesus Christ, hasten to help us!*
> *We implore you by the Holy Word of God, hasten to help us!*
> *We implore you by the heart of Our Lord Jesus Christ, hasten to help us!*
> *We implore you in the name of God's love for us, the poor, hasten to help us!*
> *We implore you in the name of God's faithfulness to us, the poor, hasten to help us!*
> *We implore you in the name of God's mercy toward us, the poor, hasten to help us!*
> *We implore you in the name of Mary, the Mother of God and our Mother, hasten to help us!*
> *We implore you by your warfare for the Kingdom of God, hasten to help us!*
> *We implore you, show us the way to the gate of life, the open heart of Our Lord!*
> *We implore you, guide us safely to the heavenly Father's House!*
> *All you nine choirs of blessed spirits, hasten to help us!*

St. Michael, the Archangel, Prince of the heavenly hosts, conqueror of the infernal dragon, you received from God the strength and power to destroy with humility the pride of the powers of darkness. We implore you, help us to true humility of heart, to unshakable fidelity to fulfill always the will of God, and to fortitude in sufferings and trials. Help us to stand before the judgment seat of God!

St. Raphael, the Archangel, arrow and medicine of Divine love, wound our hearts, we implore you, with the burning love of God and let this wound never heal, so that even in daily life we might always remain upon the path of love and overcome all things through love!

Help us, great and holy brothers, fellow-servants before God!

Protect us from ourselves, from our own cowardice and tepidity, from our self-seeking and avarice, from our envy and mistrust, from our craving for satiation, comfort, and recognition.

Free us from the bonds of sin and attachment to worldly things.

Set the goad of holy restlessness for God in our hearts, so that we never cease to seek God with longing contrition and love!

OUR INVISIBLE COMPANION

(By St. Padre Pio)

"Oh! For goodness' sake, don't forget this invisible companion, ever present, ever disposed to listen to us and even more ready to console us. Oh, wonderful intimacy! Oh, blessed companionship! If only we could understand it! Keep him always before your mind's eye. Remember this angel's presence often, thank him, pray to him, always keep up a good relationship. Open yourself up to him and confide your suffering to him. Be always afraid of offending the purity of his gaze. Know this, and keep it well present in your mind. He is easily offended, very sensitive. Turn to him in moments of supreme anguish and you will experience his beneficent help."

Prayers of Adoration and Intercession

The Pardon Prayer

My God, I believe, I adore, I trust, and I love You! I beg pardon for those who do not believe, do not adore, do not trust, and do not love You.

Angel's Prayer

O Most Holy Trinity, Father, Son, and Holy Spirit, I adore You profoundly. I offer You the most precious Body, Blood, Soul, and Divinity of Jesus Christ, present in all the tabernacles of the world, in reparation for the outrages, sacrifices, and indifference of which He is offended. By the infinite merits of the Sacred Heart of Jesus and the Immaculate Heart of Mary, I beg the conversion of poor sinners.

Sacrifice Prayer

O Jesus, it is for love of You, for the conversion of sinners, and in reparation for the sins committed against the Immaculate Heart of Mary.

A Thankful Heart

Thanksgiving was a key way St. Faustina praised Jesus. She thanked Him in everything because she trusted Him.

Jesus said to St. Faustina: "Be grateful for the smallest of My graces, because your gratitude compels Me to grant you new graces ..." (1701).

Litany of Praise

Praise You, Jesus, You are my Life, my Love.
Praise You, Jesus, You are the Lord of lords.
Praise You, Jesus, You are Christ, the King.

Praise You, Jesus, You are the King of Creation.
Praise You, Jesus, You are the Light of the World.
Praise You, Jesus, You are the Way for our Life.
Praise You, Jesus, You are the only Truth.
Praise You, Jesus, You are the Prince of Peace.
Praise You, Jesus, You are the Living Word.
Praise You, Jesus, You are our Redeemer.
Praise You, Jesus, You are the Messiah.
Praise You, Jesus, You are the Good Shepherd.
Praise You, Jesus, You are the Rock of all ages.
Praise You, Jesus, You are our Fortress.
Praise You, Jesus, You are our Victory.
Praise You, Jesus, You are our Salvation.
Praise You, Jesus, You are our Wisdom.
Praise You, Jesus, You are the Great I AM.
Praise You, Jesus, You are our Joy.
Praise You, Jesus, You are my Defense.
Praise You, Jesus, You are my Protector.
Praise You, Jesus, You are my Provider.
Praise You, Jesus, You are all that I need.
Praise You, Jesus, You are all that I want.
Praise You, Jesus, You are our Strength.
Praise You, Jesus, You are the Almighty.
Praise You, Jesus, You are the Alpha and Omega.
Praise You, Jesus, You are the Savior of the World.

"Once when I was praying fervently … I came before the throne of God. I saw a great and inaccessible light, and I saw a place destined for me, close to God. But what it was like I do not know, because a cloud covered it. However, my Guardian Angel said to me, "Here is your throne, for your faithfulness in fulfilling the will of God." (683)

APPENDIX 1

ST. FAUSTINA, MODEL OF CONVERSION

St. Faustina was willing to suffer and sacrifice for the conversion of sinners: for dying sinners, impenitent sinners, hardened sinners, and those who have lost hope in God's mercy. We, too, are invited by Jesus to offer our prayers, sufferings, and sacrifices, uniting them to His sufferings. Remember, we are doing this for our family, friends, enemies, those souls who are in danger, and the suffering souls in purgatory.

Here are some examples of how St. Faustina strived in daily conversion:

O Jesus my Lord, help me. Let what You have planned before all ages happen to me. I am ready at each beckoning of Your holy will. Enlighten my mind that I may know Your will. O God, You who pervade my soul, You know that I desire nothing but Your glory. (650)

It is no easy thing to bear sufferings joyfully, especially those which are unmerited. Fallen nature rebels, and although the intellect and will are above suffering, because they are able to do good to those who inflict suffering on them, nevertheless the emotions raise a lot of noise and, like restless spirits, attack the intellect and will. But when they see they cannot do anything by themselves, they quiet down and submit to the intellect and will. Like some kind of hideousness, they rush in and stir up a row, bent on making one obey them alone so long as they are not curbed by the intellect and will. (1152)

O you small, everyday sacrifices, you are to me like wild flowers which I strew over the feet of my beloved Jesus. I sometimes compare these trifles to the heroic virtues, and that is because their enduring nature demands heroism. (208)

I accept sweetness and bitterness with the same equanimity. One and the other will pass away. All that I keep in my soul is the love of God. For this I strive; all else is secondary. (1245)

In the sufferings of soul or body, I try to keep silence, for then my spirit gains the strength that flows from the Passion of Jesus. (487)

Today, I experienced a great suffering during the visit of our sisters. I learned of something that hurt me terribly, but I controlled myself so that the sisters didn't notice anything. For some time, the pain was tearing my heart apart, but all that is for the sake of poor sinners.... O Jesus, for poor sinners.... Jesus, my strength, stay close to me, help me.... (875)

———

[Jesus:] My pupil, have great love for those who cause you suffering. Do good to those who hate you. (1628)

[St. Faustina:] O my Master, You see very well that I feel no love for them, and that troubles me. (1628)

[Jesus:] It is not always within your power to control your feelings. You will recognize that you have love if, after having experienced annoyance and contradiction, you do not lose your peace, but pray for those who have made you suffer and wish them well. (1628)

Two Basic Ways to Help Your Loved Ones

Arise, cry out in the night,
    at the beginning of the watches!
Pour out your heart like water
    before the presence of the Lord!
Lift up your hands to him
    for the lives of your children....

— LAMENTATIONS 2:19

It's not uncommon for parents to grieve over choices their late-teen or adult children make — but those sons and daughters always have free will.

Just as God doesn't force them to believe in Him or to live a life based on Christ's teachings, neither can you.

The same holds true for the choices, actions, and beliefs of your spouse, siblings, parents, and friends.

You want to help them, but what can you do? Two basic — sometimes seemingly small, but always oh-so-powerful — ways:

1. Love them.

2. Pray for them.

A Prayer for Those Who Have Drifted from the Lord

Lord, You became a human and by Your suffering obtained salvation for all of us. Look graciously on those dearest to my heart and others who have drifted from You and the Faith. Grant them the grace to see how much You love and care for them so that they may return to You. Help me refrain from judging or criticizing them but — by my prayers and acts of kindness — gently invite them back to You and Your Church. Amen.

A Prayer to Our Lord and Our Lady for the Disillusioned

Dear Lord, please be near all those who are disillusioned, who have fallen away from You, who have never been aware of their hearts being touched by Your grace. May they find the truth, love, comfort, and consolation that only You can give.

Dear Blessed Mother Mary, pray for us — sinners, all — that we may faithfully follow your instructions and do whatever your son tells us to do. Amen.

Testimony of Father Dan Cambra, M.I.C.

That Simple, Little Prayer: A Conversion Story

When I was seven and preparing for First Holy Communion, I asked my dad why he went to Sunday Mass but never received Communion.

He said, "You're too young. You wouldn't understand."

When I was twelve and preparing for Confirmation, I again asked my dad why he went to Sunday Mass but never received Communion.

He said, "You're too young. You wouldn't understand."

When I was eighteen, I attended the diocesan seminary for my senior year of high school. In mid-December, I came home for the holidays and, thinking I had a solution, asked my dad why he didn't just go to confession so he could receive Communion with the rest of the family on Christmas.

Problem solved. Or so I thought.

"You're too young," he said yet again. "You wouldn't understand."

I left the seminary after that one year, spent my early adulthood the way a lot of young men spend theirs (enough said), and eventually found my way and entered the Marians of the Immaculate Conception.

I had never heard of St. Faustina or Divine Mercy, but an assistant novice master kept stressing the importance of this "new" devotion. I kept nodding and ignoring the saint, the devotion, and him.

And then …

When I was preparing for the deaconate, I started reading the Divine Mercy message on my own. Reading and re-reading paragraphs 186 and 187:

> Today Jesus said to me, I desire that you know more profoundly the love that burns in My Heart for souls, and you will understand this when you meditate upon My Passion. Call upon My mercy on behalf of sinners; I desire their salvation. When you say this prayer, with a contrite heart and with faith on behalf of some sinner, I will give him the grace of conversion. This is the prayer:

> "O Blood and Water, which gushed forth from the Heart of Jesus as a fount of Mercy for us, I trust in You."

I began praying it often. And then more frequently. And, finally … not all the time but it seemed like almost all the time as my ordination to the priesthood got closer and closer.

You can guess where this story is going. And you're right.

Meanwhile, on the home front, Mom mentioned to our pastor that I was going to be ordained soon and he asked why Dad was at Mass every Sunday but never received Communion. She told him Dad had received at their wedding Mass but not since then.

Later the pastor and my father spent time talking and, eventually, Dad went to confession and began receiving Communion every Sunday.

Mom, so very pleased, called to tell me he'd be doing just that at my ordination Mass.

Since then I've continued to say this short, powerful prayer for the conversion of specific friends and family members. Others have asked me to say it for the conversion of their loved ones.

It would be hard for me to list all the people I've witnessed experience a "simple" conversion or, more frequently, a profound one, including some who have overcome drug or alcohol addiction.

My assistant novice master from so many years ago — God bless his soul! — had been right.

This "new" devotion, this "new" message, this "little" prayer is more than life-changing. It's eternal-life-changing.

Examination of Conscience Based on the Seven Capital Sins

O Jesus, shield me with Your mercy and also judge me leniently.... (1093)

A cornerstone of personal conversion is becoming better at honestly looking at myself and seeing where, and how, I fall short of the mark. It is to examine how my choices, how my sins (whether big or small), are keeping me from moving toward the place God is leading me: to the person He is calling me to be, to the person He created me to be.

Pride

Can I be gracious and admit I made a mistake or I was wrong? Do I acknowledge that I have sinned against God and others and work to make amends? Do I lean toward a me-me-me attitude?

Lord, make me HUMBLE so that I love you first and my neighbor as myself.

———

O my Jesus, when shall we look upon souls with higher motives in mind? When will our judgments be true? You give us occasions to practice deeds of mercy, and instead we use the occasions to pass judgment. (1269)

When I was left alone with the Blessed Virgin, She instructed me concerning the interior life. She said, The soul's true greatness is in loving God and in humbling oneself in His presence, completely forgetting oneself and believing oneself to be nothing, because the Lord is great, but He is well-pleased only with the humble, He always opposes the proud. (1711)

Greed

Do I share with others, particularly those in need? Do I have, and want, more than I need? Do I look at possessions or wealth as a sign of virtue? When only God is watching, am I still generous? Do I give the things I value to others and to God? Do I spend money on what could — wisely and generously — be spent elsewhere?

Lord, make me GENEROUS so that I readily share what I have with others.

On another occasion the instruction I received was this: "Act in such a way that all those who come in contact with you will go away joyful. Sow happiness about you because you have received much from God; give, then, generously to others. They should take leave of you with their hearts filled with joy, even if they have no more than touched the hem of your garment. Keep well in mind the words I am telling you right now." (55)

Lust

Do I want pleasure for myself, no matter the cost to others, no matter what it may do to my soul? Do I take my marriage vows, or living chastely, seriously? Do I rationalize that "small" sins of impurity "aren't so bad"?

Lord, make me PURE of heart, mind, and body.

———

... Jesus gave me to know for what sins He subjected Himself to the scourging: these are sins of impurity. Oh, how dreadful was Jesus' moral suffering during the scourging! Then Jesus said to me, Look and see the human race in its present condition. (445)

Anger

Do I give people the benefit of the doubt before I get angry? Is anger my "default response" to anything, or anyone, I don't like? Do I try to control my temper or always offer excuses, saying, "That's just the way I am"? If I make a mistake, am I able to forgive myself?

Lord, make me MEEK in controlling my temper. Help me be like You: "slow to anger and abounding in steadfast love" (Ps 103:8).

———

...cleanse my tongue that I may not injure my neighbor with it. (375)

Jesus gave me to know the depth of His meekness and humility and to understand that He clearly demanded the same of me. (758)

I have learned that the greatest power is hidden in patience. I see that patience always leads to victory, although not immediately; but that victory will become manifest after many years. Patience is linked to meekness. (1514)

Gluttony

Do I eat more than I should, more than I need? Do I ignore my health to satisfy cravings for favorite foods? Is food my "drug of choice"?

Lord, make me TEMPERATE in all things, except in wanting to love You more.

—

Now I understand well that what unites our soul most closely to God is self-denial; that is, joining our will to the will of God. This is what makes the soul truly free, contributes to profound recollection of the spirit, and makes all life's burdens light, and death sweet. (462)

Envy

Do I celebrate the success of others? Do I allow others to share their success with me without refocusing the conversation back to me? Can I acknowledge to myself what makes me jealous, without getting angry at myself or others?

Lord, make me PRUDENT in appreciating and using all that I have achieved.

—

Virtue without prudence is not a virtue at all. We should often pray to the Holy Spirit for this grace of prudence. (1106)

I am greatly surprised at how one can be so jealous. When I see someone else's good, I rejoice at it as if it were mine. The joy of others is my joy, and the suffering of others is my suffering, for otherwise I would not dare to commune with the Lord Jesus. The spirit of Jesus is always simple, meek, sincere; all malice, envy, and unkindness disguised under a smile of good will are clever little devils. A severe word flowing from sincere love does not wound the heart. (633)

Sloth

Am I lazy? Do I avoid doing anything I don't want to do, or doing it poorly if forced to do it? Am I an active and contributing member of my marriage, my family, and my parish?

Lord, make me ZEALOUS in helping others and doing your will.

———

On one occasion, I saw Satan hurrying about and looking for someone among the sisters, but he could find no one. I felt an interior inspiration to command him in the Name of God to confess to me what he was looking for among the sisters. And he confessed, though unwillingly, "I am looking for idle souls. [cf. Si. 33:28; Pr.12:11]." When I commanded him again in the Name of God to tell me to which souls in religious life he has the easiest access, he said, again unwillingly, "To lazy and idle souls." I took note of the fact that, at present, there were no such souls in this house. Let the toiling and tired souls rejoice. (1127)

Obstacles to Conversion

What's keeping us from a deep and authentic conversion? Just as St. Thérèse of Lisieux wrote of her "little way" to holiness, often it's the "little faults" that hold us back:

- Failing to use the virtues of faith, hope, and charity.

- Ignoring how our negative words and actions affect those around us.

- Refusing to avoid our favorite near occasions of sin.

- Vainly assuming we alone can make changes in our life, instead of wisely accepting the strength and graces God stands ready to give us.

- Giving up as soon as we fall back into old ways.

- Firmly resolving to change ... tomorrow.

Fasting for the Conversion of the Heart

So we fasted and besought our God for this,
and he listened to our entreaty.
— EZRA 8:23

... every conversion of a sinful soul demands sacrifice. (961)

———

Throughout the Old and New Testament, fasting played an important role in Jewish life and tradition. Both have many examples of fasting. According to Tradition, fasting is encouraged especially in times of great temptation or severe trials. Certain devils, said Jesus, "cannot be driven out by anything but prayer and fasting" (Mk 9:29).

But fasting has been forgotten, overlooked, and underappreciated in recent time. We need to rediscover its power to help us conquer sin.

St. Faustina fasted exhaustively. It's one of the best ways to love God and our neighbor, and it helps us say "no" to temptation by inviting the Holy Spirit into our hearts. If we are more virtuous, we will naturally be kinder to our neighbor. Fasting also (it's a little funny to say) "adds weight" to our prayer intentions, so if we are praying and fasting for others, we are loving our neighbor. If we offer up our sufferings and our sacrifices, we are loving our neighbor. If we pray and fast for the holy souls in purgatory, we are loving our neighbor.

Fasting is a means to conversion. It:

- Eliminates the excesses of our life in order to make more room for God.
- Leads us more readily toward a life of inner union with God and with the heavenly world.
- Frees us from the burdens and attachments of material things.
- Strengthens and stabilizes us and helps us develop self-control, one of the fruits of the Holy Spirit.
- Helps us to recognize our weakness and dependence on God.
- Encourages us to be poor in spirit.
- Edifies our interior life.

Simply put: our souls — and our world — need fasting.

A Prayer of Thanksgiving for the Gift of Fasting

Thank you, dear Lord, for giving me the gift of fasting.
Thank you for this way for me to rid myself of bad habits.

Thank you for this way for me to be more open to Your grace and to better serve You.

Thank you for this way for me to be stronger when I face life's trials and temptations.

Thank you for this way for me to move closer to You today as You gently transform my heart, my mind, and my soul through the small sacrifices I make. Amen.

ST. BASIL ON FASTING

"There is both a physical and a spiritual fast. In the physical fast, the body abstains from food and drink. In the spiritual fast, the faster abstains from evil intentions, words, and deeds. One who truly fasts abstains from anger, rage, malice, and vengeance. One who truly fasts abstains from idle and foul talk, empty rhetoric, slander, condemnation, flattery, lying and all manner of spiteful talk, in a word, a real faster is one who withdraws from all evil.... As much as you subtract from the body, so much you will add the strength of the soul.... [B]y fasting, it is possible both to be delivered from future evils, and to enjoy good things to come."

Steps for Growing Together with Your Guardian Angel

From the Opus Angelorum Society:

- Cultivate a great esteem for the truths of our faith.

- Read Scripture every day.

- Make everything you do a sacrifice of love for God.

- Form and purify your conscience.

- Be prompt in fulfilling your duties of your state in life. If we are faithful in little things, greater gifts and lights will be given to us.

- Order your "steps" in the footsteps of Our Lord. On the tomb of a Prior of the Order of the Holy Cross was written the epitaph: "He never took a step that was not directed to the honor of God." When his body was exhumed, the investigators discovered his legs were incorrupt. It is a battle against character faults, habitual venial sins, concessions to comfort, to human respect. Those who are shy of sacrifice will never develop a deep friendship with their angel.

- Make an effort to be genuinely kind and patient. Kindness is the trait of generous love that willingly exceeds the demands of justice. It is a divine virtue. Patience, "hard thing," is literally the willingness to suffer.

- Walk constantly in the presence of God and your angel.

- Rejoice in the Love of the Father, in Christ's personal love for YOU, in the sanctifying, loving presence of the Holy Spirit. Reflect frequently upon Our Lord's love for you, upon His insatiable thirst to be able to communicate Himself more perfectly to you. Let your heart be enkindled with the Love of Mary, your Mother, and the love of your guardian angel.

The St. Gertrude Prayer

Eternal Father, I offer Thee the most precious Blood of Thy Divine Son, Jesus, in union with the Masses said throughout the world today, for all the holy souls in purgatory, for sinners everywhere, for sinners in the universal Church, those in my own home and within my family. Amen.

Offering the Heroic Act of Charity

This act consists in offering to the Divine Majesty for the souls in purgatory all the satisfactions of our works and our indulgences throughout life, as well as all the suffrages that shall be offered for us after death. It is a worthy custom to make this offering through the hands of the Blessed Virgin, that she may apply our satisfaction as she sees fit for the release of the souls in purgatory. Those who make this act gain for themselves special merits and the particular blessing of God.

———

O Heavenly Father, in union with the merits of Jesus and Mary, I offer You, for the holy souls in purgatory, all the works of satisfaction of my entire life, as well as all the satisfactory works that will be offered for me after my death. These works I surrender into the most pure hands of the Immaculate Virgin Mary, that she may apply them to souls which, according to her wisdom and motherly love, should be first delivered from purgatory. Graciously accept, O my God, this offering, and may it win for me your constant favor. Amen.

The Role of Sacramentals

Sacramentals are sacred signs instituted by the Church.
They prepare men to receive the fruit of the sacraments and sanctify different circumstances of life.
— CATECHISM OF THE CATHOLIC CHURCH (N. 1677)

———

- **The Holy Rosary:** Our Lady tells us in multiple approved apparitions to pray the Rosary daily for personal conversion and the "conversion of sinners."

- **Miraculous Medal:** Marie Alphonse Ratisbonne, an anti-Catholic Jew, befriended a baron in Rome and began wearing the Miraculous Medal as a simple test. On January 20, 1842, while waiting for the baron in the church of Sant'Andrea delle Fratte, Ratisbonne encountered a vision of the Blessed Virgin Mary. He converted to Catholicism, joined the priesthood, and began a ministry for the conversion of Jews.

- **Green Scapular:** Ten years after the manifestation of the Miraculous Medal to St. Catherine Labouré, the Blessed Virgin Mary (on September 8, 1840, the feast of her nativity) entrusted the Green Scapular of her Immaculate Heart to Sister Justine Bisqueyburu, a religious of the Daughters of Charity of St. Vincent de Paul. Our Lady promised that this new scapular would contribute to the conversion of souls, particularly those who have no faith, and would procure for them a happy death.

The Use of Holy Water

Holy Water is indeed of great help to the dying. (601)

———

Holy water is a sacramental that remits venial sin. Because of the blessing attached to it, Holy Mother Church strongly urges its use upon her children, especially when dangers threaten, such as fire, storms, sickness, and other calamities. Every home should have a supply of holy water, which:

- **Makes prayers effective:** Prayers ascend to heaven each time you take holy water and sprinkle a drop either for yourself or for another, whether he be present or absent — and God's blessings descend on soul and body. Holy water recalls our baptism and is a sign of repentance of sin.

- **Protects us against evil:** The devil hates holy water because of its power over him. He cannot long abide in a place or near a person that is often sprinkled with this blessed water.

- **Aids your dear ones who live at a distance:** Holy water, sprinkled with faith and piety, can move the Sacred Heart to bless your loved ones and protect them from all harm of soul and body. When worry and fear take possession of your heart, hasten to your holy water font, and give your dear ones the benefit of the Church's prayers.

THE POWER OF HOLY WATER

In her autobiography, St. Teresa of Ávila wrote:

"I was once in an oratory, and [the devil] appeared to me in an abominable form at my left side. Because he spoke to me, I looked particularly at his mouth — which was most frightening. It seemed that a great flame, all bright without shadow, came forth from his body. He told me in a terrifying way that I had really freed myself from his hands but that he would catch me with them again. I was struck with great fear and blessed myself as best I could; he disappeared, but returned right away. This happened to me twice. I didn't know what to do. There was some holy water there, and I threw it in that direction; he never returned again. ... I often experience that there is nothing the devils flee from more — without returning — than holy water." (Chapter 31)

Upon the testimony of such a great saint, we see the importance not only of pausing to bless ourselves with holy water as we enter and leave church but also of having holy water available in our homes.

- **Refreshes the holy souls:** Only in purgatory can one understand how ardently a poor soul longs for holy water. If we desire to make a host of intercessors for ourselves, let us try to realize now some of their yearnings, and never forget them at the holy water font. The holy souls nearest to heaven may need the sprinkling of only one drop to relieve their pining souls.

- **Remits venial sins:** Because holy water is one of the Church's sacramentals, it remits venial sin. Keep your soul beautifully pure in God's sight by making the Sign of the Cross carefully while saying: "By this holy water and by Your precious Blood, wash away all my sins, O Lord."

APPENDIX 2

THE CATECHISM OF THE CATHOLIC CHURCH ON CONVERSION

Why a Sacrament of Reconciliation After Baptism?

1426 *Conversion to Christ*, the new birth of Baptism, the gift of the Holy Spirit and the Body and Blood of Christ received as food have made us "holy and without blemish," just as the Church herself, the Bride of Christ, is "holy and without blemish." Nevertheless the new life received in Christian initiation has not abolished the frailty and weakness of human nature, nor the inclination to sin that tradition calls *concupiscence*, which remains in the baptized such that with the help of the grace of Christ they may prove themselves in the struggle of Christian life. This is the struggle of *conversion* directed toward holiness and eternal life to which the Lord never ceases to call us. [Emphasis in original.]

Interior Penance

1430 Jesus' call to conversion and penance, like that of the prophets before him, does not aim first at outward works, "sackcloth and ashes," fasting and mortification, but at the *conversion of the heart, interior conversion*. Without this, such penances remain sterile and false; however, interior conversion urges expression in visible signs, gestures and works of penance. [Emphasis in original.]

1431 Interior repentance is a radical reorientation of our whole life, a return, a conversion to God with all our heart, an end of sin, a turning away from evil, with repugnance toward the evil actions we have committed. At the same time it entails the desire and resolution to change one's life, with hope in God's mercy and trust in the help of his grace. This conversion of heart is accompanied by a salutary pain and sadness which the Fathers called *animi cruciatus* (affliction of spirit) and *compunctio cordis* (repentance of heart).

1432 The human heart is heavy and hardened. God must give man a new heart. Conversion is first of all a work of the grace of God who makes our hearts return to him: "Restore us to thyself, O LORD, that we may be restored!" God gives us the strength to begin anew. It is in discovering the greatness of God's love that our heart is shaken by the horror and weight of sin and begins to fear offending God by sin and being separated from him. The human heart is converted by looking upon him whom our sins have pierced:

> Let us fix our eyes on Christ's blood and understand how precious it is to his Father, for, poured out for our salvation, it has brought to the whole world the grace of repentance.

1433 Since Easter, the Holy Spirit has proved "the world wrong about sin," i.e., proved that the world has not believed in him whom the Father has sent. But this same Spirit who brings sin to light is also the Consoler who gives the human heart grace for repentance and conversion.

The Many Forms of Penance in Christian Life

1434 The interior penance of the Christian can be expressed in many and various ways. Scripture and the Fathers insist above all on three forms, *fasting*, *prayer*, and *almsgiving*, which express conversion in relation to oneself, to God, and to others. Alongside the radical purification brought about by Baptism or martyrdom they cite as means of obtaining forgiveness of sins: efforts at reconciliation with one's neighbor, tears of repentance, concern for the salvation of one's neighbor, the intercession of the saints, and the practice of charity "which covers a multitude of sins." [Emphasis in original.]

1435 Conversion is accomplished in daily life by gestures of reconciliation, concern for the poor, the exercise and defense of justice and right, by the admission of faults to one's brethren, fraternal correction, revision of life, examination of conscience, spiritual direction, acceptance of suffering, endurance of persecution for the sake of righteousness. Taking up one's cross each day and following Jesus is the surest way of penance.

1436 *Eucharist and Penance.* Daily conversion and penance find their source and nourishment in the Eucharist, for in it is made present the sacrifice of Christ which has reconciled us with God. Through the Eucharist those who live from the life of Christ are fed and strengthened. "It is a remedy to free us from our daily faults and to preserve us from mortal sins." [Emphasis in original.]

1437 Reading Sacred Scripture, praying the Liturgy of the Hours and the Our Father — every sincere act of worship or devotion revives the spirit of conversion and repentance within us and contributes to the forgiveness of our sins.

1438 *The seasons and days of penance* in the course of the liturgical year (Lent, and each Friday in memory of the death of the Lord) are intense moments of the Church's penitential practice. These times are particularly appropriate for spiritual exercises, penitential liturgies, pilgrimages as signs of penance, voluntary self-denial such as fasting and almsgiving, and fraternal sharing (charitable and missionary works). [Emphasis in original.]

Bibliography and Acknowledgments

Kieninger, Father Titus, O.R.C. *The Angels in the Diary of Saint Faustina Kowalska.* Carrollton, OH: Order of the Holy Cross, Inc., 2014.

Kosicki, George, W., C.S.B. *Now Is the Time for Mercy, Revised Edition.* Stockbridge, MA: Marian Press, 2011.

———. *Revelations of Divine Mercy: Daily Readings from the Diary of Blessed Faustina Kowalska.* Copyright © 1996 by The Congregation of Marians of the Immaculate Conception of the Blessed Virgin Mary. Ann Arbor, MI: Servant Publications, 1996.

———. *Thematic Concordance to the Diary of St. Maria Faustina Kowalska.* Stockbridge, MA: Marian Press, 2015.

———, with David Came. *Faustina, Saint for Our Times: A Personal Look at Her Life, Spirituality, and Legacy.* Stockbridge, MA: Marian Press, 2011.

Kowalska, St. Maria Faustina. *Diary of Saint Maria Faustina Kowalska.* Stockbridge, MA: Marian Press, 1987.

Martin, Ralph, *The Fulfillment of All Desires.* Steubenville, OH: Emmaus Road Publishing, 2006.

Monks of St. Meinrad Archabbey, The. *The Tradition of Catholic Prayer.* Collegeville, MN: Liturgical Press, 2007.

Opus Sanctorum Angelorum. Newsletter (Summer 1993). Copyright © Confraternity of Priests in Opus Angelorum.

Tarnawska, Maria. *Sister Faustina Kowalska: Her Life and Mission.* Stockbridge, MA: Marian Press, 2000.

Resources

For information about the National Shrine of the Divine Mercy and becoming a Friend of Mercy, go to www.thedivinemercy.org.

Association of Marian Helpers
Eden Hill
Stockbridge, MA 01263

Holy Souls Sodality
c/o Association of Marian Helpers
Eden Hill
Stockbridge, MA 01263
www.prayforsouls.org

St. Monica Sodality
A devotion promoting prayer and self-mortification for the return to the Catholic Faith of family members and friends. The core of the Sodality Devotion is weekly recitation of the St. Monica Novena, followed by the Holy Rosary for all of the intentions submitted to the Sodality.

For information contact:

St. John Cantius Church
825 N. Carpenter Street
Chicago, IL 60642

For memberships, and to obtain Masses and Gregorian Masses:

Pious Union of St. Joseph
953 East Michigan Avenue
Grass Lake, MI 49240
517-522-8017
www.pusj.org

———

The following prayers are adapted from and used with permission of the Order of Canons Regular of the Holy Cross, Carrollton, OH:

- Litany of Longing
- Supplication to the Angels
- Steps Toward Growing Together with Your Guardian Angel

For more information contact:

Opus Sanctorum Angelorum
164 Apollo Road SE
Carrollton, OH 44615
www.opusangelorum.org

ABOUT THE COVER

I invite you to use the image on the cover as inspiration for your meditation, for your transformation, and for the conversion of sinners.

The merciful Jesus welcomes the wayward young man, who is in a terrible state. His clothes are tattered, no sandals cover his blistered feet, his hair has not been groomed for weeks, and who knows how long it has been since he bathed.

In spite of the disfigured features of this young man, Jesus welcomes him back with open arms. The Lord also welcomes us back into His loving arms when we "return with a humble and contrite heart."

The moment of conversion takes place when we recognize our sinfulness, our nothingness, and our corruption without the grace of God and make the move to "return" to the loving arms of Our Lord.

May this book open your heart, mind, and soul to aid you to convert, turn around, and return to God our Father, with Jesus Christ, His merciful Son, by the power and inspiration of the Holy Spirit.

— FATHER C. FRANK PHILLIPS, CR
Pastor and Superior of the Canons Regular of St. John Cantius

ABOUT THE AUTHOR

Susan Tassone has long been a passionate champion for the holy souls in purgatory and is recognized as leading a worldwide "purgatory movement."

The author of nine best-sellers, including *St. Faustina Prayer Book for the Holy Souls in Purgatory*, Susan makes speaking appearances throughout the country. She's a frequent and popular guest on national radio and television programs as well as social media. In 2013, she was featured in the groundbreaking documentary *Purgatory: The Forgotten Church.*

She also continues to work tirelessly to raise donations for Masses for the holy souls.

Susan holds a master's degree in religious education from Loyola University Chicago and had the honor and privilege of being granted two private audiences with St. John Paul II, who bestowed a special blessing on her and her ministry for the holy souls.

Learn more at: susantassone.com.

Other Books by Susan Tassone

The Rosary for the Holy Souls in Purgatory: This little book slips easily into your pocket, so it can go with you anywhere you have time to pray. Make praying for the holy souls a regular part of your devotional life. **ID# T25**

Thirty-Day Devotions for the Holy Souls: This book offers comfort to those who are grieving and gives them a personal and powerful method of praying for their departed family member or friend. **ID# T103**

The Way of the Cross for the Holy Souls in Purgatory: This one-of-a-kind combination of the traditional prayers of the Stations of the Cross and scriptural reflections focuses on Christ's passion and death. **ID# T192**

Praying with the Saints for the Holy Souls in Purgatory: This inspiring book shows how you can join the saints in this act of divine charity, thereby attaining spiritual gifts for acts done for the souls that cry out to us for relief. **ID# T833**

Prayers, Promises, and Devotions for the Holy Souls in Purgatory: Become a prayer warrior on behalf of the suffering souls in purgatory, and bring comfort to them and to yourself along the way. **ID# T1254**

Day by Day for the Holy Souls in Purgatory: 365 Reflections: Every day we have another opportunity to pray for the holy souls in purgatory, and Susan gives you a unique tool to do just that. **ID# T1577**

St. Faustina Prayer Book for the Holy Souls in Purgatory: Susan turns to a passionate and powerful guide to help us pray for the holy souls in purgatory, St. Faustina Kowalska. Includes devotions, prayers, novenas, and the wisdom of St. Faustina. **ID# T1759**